THE HOLDOVERS

Written by

David Hemingson

> MISS CRANE
> Christmas cookies. I made them for
> the faculty. Well, not all the
> faculty. Anyway, these are for
> you.

She smiles, lipstick on her teeth. He takes the plate, nods and closes the door.

"TIME HAS COME TODAY" by The Chambers Brothers crackles onto the soundtrack as we go to --

INT. STUDENT DORMITORY - HALLWAY - DAY

The song blares from a portable record player as a scrum of Boys shout and shove, dressing -- oxford, tie, blazer -- as they get ready to go home. One emerges from the shower at the end of the hall.

INT. STUDENT DORMITORY - DORM ROOM - DAY

ANGUS TULLY, 17, hurriedly packs the suitcase atop his bed. He retrieves a PHOTOGRAPH from his nightstand drawer and slips it into his suitcase.

Knucklehead DOUG CRANDALL approaches, brushing his teeth, and plucks a BLACK SPEEDO from the suitcase.

> CRANDALL
> Hey, Tully, what're you doing with
> women's underwear?

> ANGUS
> (snatching it back)
> It's the same swimsuit James Bond
> wears in "On Her Majesty's Secret
> Service." Can't get more masculine
> than that.

> CRANDALL
> Why don't you just wear cut-offs?

Crandall spits in the sink. Angus rinses it away.

> ANGUS
> 'Cause I'm going to St. Kitts. I'm
> not going to be the only dickhead
> on the beach in cut-offs.

                    CRANDALL
          Oooh, look out everyone. Tully's
          going to St. Kitts. They still
          look like panties.

Crandall walks away, still brushing his teeth.

                    ANGUS
          Yeah, you're right, Crandall, you
          caught me. It's your mother's
          panties. Tell her thanks for the
          good times.

Hostile TEDDY KOUNTZE, 16, comes by in his robe.

                    KOUNTZE
          Hey, Tully, where are my
          cigarettes?

                    ANGUS
          Your cigarettes?

                    KOUNTZE
          You stole my fucking cigarettes.

                    ANGUS
          I resent that baseless accusation.

                    KOUNTZE
          Cut the shit. I have no
          cigarettes, and Briggs says you
          suddenly have five of them to trade
          for a skin mag.

                    ANGUS
          I don't indulge in pornography. I
          get enough of the real thing.
          Especially with Crandall's mom!

HANS HARRIMAN approaches with a small bag of pot.

                    HARRIMAN
          Kountze, ten dollars is too much for
          this. Looks more like a nickel bag.

                    ANGUS
          Yeah, don't buy that, Harriman. He's
          ripping you off. Plus, that's ditch
          weed.

                    KOUNTZE
          Fuck you, Tully. This shit's
          premium weed.
                    (MORE)

                    KOUNTZE (CONT'D)
          And unlike you, I'm stuck here, so
          it's gotta last me through
          Christmas.

                    ANGUS
          Yeah, take pity on him, Harriman.
          He's a poor little Christmas orphan
          with nowhere to go. Little
          Christmas orphan needs his pot and
          porn.

INT. KITCHEN - DAY

Head cook MARY LAMB leads half a dozen KITCHEN WORKERS
toiling over an industrial-sized range, stirring oatmeal,
scrambling eggs and frying bacon.

                    MARY
          Ten minutes, ladies. Ten minutes!

Mary glances up from her work to notice the snow falling
outside the window.

EXT. QUAD - DAY

Bundled up against the cold in a time-worn duffle coat, pipe
between his teeth, Paul briskly crosses the snowy campus.
Boys race past him toward the dining hall.

INT. DINING HALL - DAY

A grand room -- high ceiling, animal trophies -- teeming with
hungry boys.

AT THE MASTERS' TABLE

Professors ROSENSWEIG and ENDICOTT eat breakfast.

                    ROSENSWIEG
          I can't believe you got out of it.

                    ENDICOTT
          Luck of the Irish.

                    ROSENSWIEG
          I thought this was your year.

                    ENDICOTT
          It was. I told Woodrup my mother
          has lupus.

                    ROSENSWIEG
Does she?

                    ENDICOTT
I don't know. Probably. We don't
talk about those things.

                    ROSENSWIEG
So who's getting stuck with it?

                    ENDICOTT
Who do you think?

Endicott glances at an empty chair.

                    ROSENSWIEG
That poor walleyed bastard.

INT. HEADMASTER'S OFFICE - DAY

Large and stately. Portraits of past headmasters.

Paul stands before an acre of desk. DR. HARDY WOODRUP, late
40s, sits writing a list and smoking. His wardrobe may be
Brooks Bros, but his beard says 1970.

Paul's eyes settle on a crystal bottle of COGNAC tied with
ribbon.

                    DR. WOODRUP
                 (noticing)
Remy Martin, Louis XIII. Christmas
gift from the Board of Trustees.

                    PAUL
How generous of them.

                    DR. WOODRUP
Thank you again for doing this,
Hunham. I wouldn't have asked if
it weren't an emergency.

                    PAUL
Mr. Endicott's mother. Right.
What a tragedy.

                    DR. WOODRUP
It's not as though you had plans to
leave campus anyway. And of course
there's a nice little bonus in it
for you.

                    PAUL
          Well. *Non nobis solum nati sumus*,
          I suppose.

Woodrup looks at him.

                    PAUL (CONT'D)
          "Not for ourselves alone are we
          born."

                    DR. WOODRUP
          I'm guessing that's Cicero.

                    PAUL
          Cicero, yes. Very good, Hardy.
          You remembered.

Woodrup absorbs Paul's "praise," then finishes writing and
hands over a LIST. Paul swivels his head to read it.

                    DR. WOODRUP
          There will be just four boys
          holding over this year.

                    PAUL
          Oh yes. I know a couple of these
          reprobates.

                    DR. WOODRUP
          Let's be a little more... elastic
          in our assessment, shall we? It's
          hard enough for them to be away
          from home on the holidays.

                    PAUL
          Latitude is the last thing these
          boys need.

                    DR. WOODRUP
          Paul, at your core you're an
          excellent teacher, but your approach
          to the students is rather...
          traditional.

                    PAUL
          The school was founded in 1797. I
          thought tradition was our stock in
          trade.

                    DR. WOODRUP
          Then let's call it hidebound. You
          know, unwavering, resistant to --

                    PAUL
Yes, yes, yes - I know what
"hidebound" means. Look, I get it.
You're still angry that I failed
Jordan Osgood.

                    DR. WOODRUP
Senator Osgood was very upset when
Princeton rescinded Jordan's
acceptance, yes. And I've
continued to have to deal with the
fallout.

                    PAUL
Hardy, are we supposed to let these
boys skate by as long as daddy
builds a new gymnasium?

                    DR. WOODRUP
Of course not. That's not who we
are. But we can't be ignorant of
politics.

                    PAUL
That boy is too dumb to pour piss
out of a boot. A genuine
troglodyte.

                    DR. WOODRUP
Jesus Christ, Paul. He was a
legacy and the son of one of our
biggest donors. Ever think his dad
might be expecting a little
consideration for his dollar?

                    PAUL
And he got it -- a first-class
education for his son. Come on,
Hardy.
     (gesturing at a portrait)
As Dr. Green used to say, our one
true purpose is to produce young
men of good character --

                    DR. WOODRUP
-- I don't care what Dr. Green used
to say --

                    PAUL
-- and we cannot sacrifice our
integrity on the altar of their
entitlement.

Hardy rubs the bridge of his nose. This bullshit again.

                    PAUL (CONT'D)
I'm just trying to instill basic
academic discipline. That's my
job. Isn't it yours?

                    DR. WOODRUP
It was, until I became headmaster
and saw that it's not so simple to
keep the damned school afloat. I
begged you -- begged you -- to give
the kid a C-minus.

                    PAUL
There are instructors here who will
do that. I am not one of them.

                    DR. WOODRUP
Here's the manual and a full set of
keys. Everything you need to know
is in there. Your only task is to
ensure the boys' absolute safety
and good condition. And at least
pretend to be a human being.
Please. It's Christmas.

Paul fixes him with a sour stare.

INT. PAUL'S CLASSROOM - DAY

Ten Boys impatiently await their teacher -- among them Angus,
who checks his watch and looks --

OUT THE WINDOW

-- where JASON SMITH, 18, a handsome senior with long blonde
hair, plays catch football with a BUDDY. A half-dozen other
SENIORS, all smoking and cool as shit, look on.

                    ANGUS
Fuck this half-day bullshit! I've
got things to do. Where the hell
is Walleye?

                    KOUNTZE
Probably jerking off into the cobb
salad.

Pimply CARTER CROCKER turns to Kountze, alarmed.

                    CROCKER
Why would he do that?

                    KOUNTZE
          Because he's Walleye. Who knows
          what that foul-smelling freak does?

                    CROCKER
          But you went straight to the Cobb
          salad. I mean, do you know
          something? Because I eat the Cobb
          salad.

Paul bursts through the door, blue books in hand.

                    PAUL
          Your final exams, gentlemen.

Whistling happily, Paul drops exam after exam onto the Boys'
desks. They stare with queasy disbelief at the parade of Cs,
Ds and Fs. Angus, however, got a B+.

                    PAUL (CONT'D)
          I can tell from your faces that
          many of you are shocked at the
          outcome. I, on the other hand, am
          not. Because I have had the
          misfortune of teaching you this
          semester, and even with my ocular
          limitations, I witness firsthand
          your glazed, uncomprehending
          expressions.

                    KOUNTZE
          Sir, I don't understand.

                    PAUL
          That's glaringly apparent.

                    KOUNTZE
          It's just... I can't fail this
          class.

                    PAUL
          Don't sell yourself short, Mr.
          Kountze. I truly believe that you
          can.

                    KOUNTZE
          But I'm supposed to go to Cornell.

                    PAUL
          Unlikely.

                    KOUNTZE
          Please, sir. My father is going to
          flip out.

Panicked murmurs of agreement. Paul absorbs the squall of
emotion and draws a breath, resigned.

> PAUL
> All right. In the spirit of the
> season, I suppose the most
> constructive way of addressing your
> shortcomings is to offer a make-up
> exam. You'll all get a second run
> at this. After break.

A wave of relief washes over the room.

> PAUL (CONT'D)
> Of course, it will not be the same
> exam. You'll now be responsible
> for new material as well. Your
> grade will be an average of the
> two. Please open your books to
> chapter six. The Peloponnesian
> War, gentlemen. We've already met
> Pericles. Now meet Demosthenes.

Gasps of incredulity. What an asshole.

> ANGUS
> No offense, sir, but is this really
> the right time to start a new
> chapter? I mean, we all appreciate
> the make-up exam gesture, but our
> families are here. Most other
> teachers have already cancelled
> class. We have chapel in forty
> minutes, and then we're out of
> here. Our heads are elsewhere.

> PAUL
> And where exactly is your head, Mr.
> Tully?

> ANGUS
> I don't know. St. Kitts.

> PAUL
> Yes, I see you've brought your
> valise.

> ANGUS
> Spot on, sir. It's just that it's
> been a really exhausting semester,
> and getting into new material *now*,
> right before break? Honestly, it's
> a little absurd. Sir.

Silence, as all await Paul's response to this
insubordination.

> PAUL
> Well, I'd hate to be absurd. So
> let's scuttle the whole thing,
> shall we, and let the original
> grades stand.

Paul slams his textbook shut.

> KOUNTZE
> Excuse me, sir, I think we all
> liked the first option better.
> What'd you say the guy's name is?
> Demosta-who?

> PAUL
> Of course, I will still expect you
> to be familiar with chapter six
> upon your return, so pack those
> text books. And if displeased,
> take it up with your champion, Mr.
> Tully. Dismissed.

Paul leaves. The Boys rise. Kountze stares menacingly at
Angus, who knows he fucked up but can't show remorse.
Contrition equals weakness.

> ANGUS
> I got us out early, didn't I?

INT. CHAPEL - DAY

The mood is festive, abuzz with anticipation for the coming
holiday. Accompanied by a booming PIPE ORGAN, FATHER JOE
leads a hymn.

CLOSE-UPS of the walls, where names of alumni killed in war
are carved into stone. We end on a portrait of CURTIS EZRA
LAMB in uniform, with a plaque bearing the dates 1951-1970.

STUDENTS, PARENTS and STAFF clog the pews. Mary sits
prominently in the front row, a cardigan over her uniform.

> ALL
> ...*now Thy gracious kingdom bring.*

> FATHER JOE
> Please be seated. Welcome, Barton
> students, faculty and parents.
> (MORE)

                    FATHER JOE (CONT'D)
          I know you're all anxious to start
          the holidays -- I can see the boys
          shifting in their seats -- but
          before we release you to your
          bountiful tables and the blessings
          of family, let us pray for those
          less fortunate. Let us remember
          the poor and the helpless, the
          cold, the hungry and the
          oppressed...

ANGUS looks around for his parents. Seated just behind him,
Kountze leans forward menacingly.

                    KOUNTZE
          Extra reading over vacation and no
          make-up test? You fucking kidding
          me? Nice work, Anus.

                    ANGUS
          Can you not talk, please? I'm
          trying to pray.

                    KOUNTZE
          You better pray I don't catch you
          alone, because I will full-on nut-
          punch you.

                    ANGUS
          Tone it down. Jesus can hear you.

Paul glares at Endicott, who is seated next to him.

                    PAUL
          Sorry to hear about your mother,
          Endicott.

                    ENDICOTT
          Oh. Yes. Thank you.

                    PAUL
          We're all pulling for her.

                    FATHER JOE
          And finally let us pray for the
          soul of Curtis Lamb, Barton class
          of 1969. Just this year, Curtis
          gave his life valiantly in the
          service of his country. And let us
          again extend our deepest
          condolences to one of the most
          cherished members of the Barton
          family, his mother Mary.

Mary can barely hide a mix of powerful emotions -- grief, anger, resentment -- behind a stoic face.

                    FATHER JOE (O.S.) (CONT'D)
          Mary, we remember Curtis as such an
          outstanding and promising young
          man, and we know this holiday
          season will be especially difficult
          without him. Please know that we
          accompany you in your grief.
               (switching gears)
          May the all-powerful God, who
          protected Abraham when he left his
          native land, protect all of our
          brave soldiers until they are
          delivered safely home to us. We
          ask this through Christ our Lord,
          Amen.

                    ALL
          Amen.

                    FATHER JOE
          We wish you all a very Merry
          Christmas or, as the case may be, a
          very Happy Hanukkah.

The organ starts. All stand and surge toward the exits.

EXT. ADMINISTRATION BUILDING - DAY

SHOUTS OF JOY as boys hauling suitcases and duffel bags rush toward a line of Mercedeses, Jaguars and Cadillacs.

                    DR. WOODRUP
          Merry Christmas, everyone! Merry
          Christmas!

Angus scans the cars with growing concern.

                    OFFICE LADY
               (approaching)
          Angus Tully. Phone call.

INT. ADMINISTRATIVE OFFICE - MOMENTS LATER

Angus clutches the receiver.

                    ANGUS
          You're telling me this now?

                    JUDY (O.S.)
I'm so sorry. Sweetheart. I know
it's last minute, and I'm
absolutely heartbroken about it,
devastated really, but could you
please see your way to staying at
school over break? Just this once?
Stanley has been working so hard,
and we never had time for a
honeymoon.

                    ANGUS
You guys have been married since
July. You've had all these months.

                    JUDY (O.S.)
Something always came up. I know
it's a lot to ask, but you know how
lonely I've been.

                    ANGUS
I've been lonely, too. And what
about Boston? You promised on the
way we'd spend some time in Boston.

                    JUDY (O.S.)
Angus, listen to me. This is our
new family, okay? I know you miss
your father -- I do too -- but now
there's someone new in my life.
     (off Angus's silence)
It's just this once, darling.
We'll be together at spring break,
and we'll have the whole summer.

                    ANGUS
Fuck the summer. And fuck Stanley.

                    JUDY (O.S.)
Angus!

                    ANGUS
Are you kidding me? I'm just
supposed to stay here? Mom, don't
do this. Please.

INT. DORM COMMON ROOM - DAY

Paul addresses the holdovers. In addition to our old friend
Kountze, there are --

JASON SMITH, the long-haired senior we saw throwing a
football. Up close, he's chiseled and muscular, a heavy-
lidded Viking warrior/Zen master.

YE-JOON PARK, 15, wide-eyed and innocent.

ALEX OLLERMAN, 14, pale as a light bulb.

> PAUL
> I suspect that, just like me, this
> is not the way you want to spend
> your holidays. But such are the
> vicissitudes of life, and as Barton
> men, we learn to confront our
> challenges with heads help high and
> with a spirit of courage and good
> fellowship - in strict accordance
> with the dictates of the manual, of
> course.

Eyes red, Angus enters with his suitcase.

> PAUL (CONT'D)
> Mr. Tully. Are you joining us as
> well? What happened to St. Kitts?

> KOUNTZE
> Yeah, you had plans. Big plans.

> ANGUS
> (low)
> Something came up.

Angus drops his suitcase. Paul notes his agony but forges
on.

> PAUL
> So for the next two weeks, we'll be
> following a standard school
> schedule --

> SMITH
> Sir, we're on vacation.

> PAUL
> -- which means we'll be taking our
> meals together. And you will
> observe regular hours of study.

> KOUNTZE
> Are you kidding me?

                    PAUL
          The Peloponnesian War awaits, Mr.
          Kountze, you and Mr. Tully. The
          rest of you can get a jump on next
          semester. It'll pay off. You'll
          see.

                    ANGUS
          We're already holding over, and now
          we're being punished for it?

                    PAUL
          You will be afforded limited
          windows for recreation and
          supervised physical activity.

                    ANGUS
          The gym's not even open yet.

                    SMITH
          Yeah, they've only lacquered half
          the floor.

                    PAUL
          The fresh air will do you good.

                    ANGUS
          It's like fifteen degrees outside.

                    PAUL
          The Romans bathed naked in the
          freezing Tiber. Adversity builds
          character, Mr. Tully. Speaking of
          which, the school is cutting the
          heat to dormitories and faculty
          housing, so we'll all be bunking in
          the infirmary.

EXT. QUAD - DUSK

The boys haul their bags toward the Infirmary.

                    ANGUS
          This is the most bullshit ever. If
          we have to stay, why'd we have to
          draw Walleye?

                    SMITH
          You know he used to be a student
          here, right?

                         ANGUS
          That's why he knows how to inflict
          maximum pain on us, the sadistic
          fuck.

                         KOUNTZE
          At least we didn't draw Decker.
          He'd be perving all over us.

                         ANGUS
          Hey, guys, hold up for a second.

Angus stops to light a cigarette. Smiles at Kountze.

                         ANGUS (CONT'D)
          Want one?

                         KOUNTZE
              (glaring at him)
          No. I got something else.

Kountze grabs the lighter from Angus and sparks a joint.
Ollerman and Park look at each other, terrified.

                         ANGUS
          Hey, don't smoke that out here. I
          don't want to get busted by
          Walleye.

                         KOUNTZE
          Don't be such a pussy.

                         ANGUS
          I'm not a pussy. I just don't want
          to end up at Fork Union paying for
          your mistake.

Kountze ignores him and pulls hard on the joint.

                         KOUNTZE
              (to Smith)
          Hey. Teddy Kountze.

                         SMITH
          Jason Smith.

                         KOUNTZE
          I know who you are. Want to hit
          this?

Smith looks around. The coast is clear.

                         SMITH
          Uh, yeah.

Smith takes a toke.

                    KOUNTZE
          You got a great arm, man.

                    SMITH
          Yeah, well, it's just football.

                    KOUNTZE
          How'd you get stuck holding over?

                    SMITH
          I'm supposed to be skiing with my
          folks up at Haystack, but my dad
          put his foot down. Said I can't
          come home unless I cut my hair.

                    ANGUS
          So why don't you cut your hair?

                    SMITH
          Civil disobedience, man.

                    ANGUS
          Yeah, right.

                    SMITH
          No, he's cool. It's just a battle
          of wills. Still, I was hoping he'd
          cave first, because the powder up
          at Haystack is so sweet right now.

                    KOUNTZE
               (to Park)
          What about you, Mr. Moto? Why are
          you here?

                    YE-JOON
          No, my name is Ye-Joon. My family
          is in Korea, and they think it's
          too far to me to travel alone.

                    KOUNTZE
          I figured it was because your
          rickshaw was broken.

                    YE-JOON
          What's a rickshaw?

                    ANGUS
          You're an asshole, Kountze. Your
          mind's a cesspool and a shallow one
          at that. Shallow.

                    KOUNTZE
          Who's the asshole, Tully? You're
          the one who blew up history.

                    SMITH
               (to Ollerman)
          Hey, you. What's your story, man?

                    OLLERMAN
          Alex Ollerman. I'm here because my
          parents are on mission in Paraguay.
          We're LDS.

                    SMITH
          Mormons, right?

                    KOUNTZE
          Don't you guys wear some kind of
          magic underwear?

                    OLLERMAN
          Common misconception. Actually, it's
          called a temple garment, and we're
          only supposed to wear it when --

                    KOUNTZE
          Hey, what's with the townies?

Kountze has just spotted TWO MEN in hunter's orange emerging
from the chapel -- with the Christmas tree.

                    ANGUS
          Excuse me! What are you doing with
          our Christmas tree?

                    TOWNIE #1
          The school sold it back to us.
          Scotch pine, still fresh.

                    TOWNIE #2
          Yeah, we're gonna put it back on
          the lot. Do it every year.

                    ANGUS
          This is the most bullshit ever.

INT. KITCHEN - DUSK

Mary has a smoke and a drink at a small table in the back.
Paul enters.

                    PAUL
          Hello, Mary.

                    MARY
          Mr. Hunham. I heard you got stuck
          babysitting this year. How'd you
          manage that?

                    PAUL
          Oh, I don't know. I suppose I
          failed someone who richly deserved
          it.

                    MARY
          The Osgood kid? Yeah, he was a
          real asshole. Rich and dumb.
          Popular combination around here.

                    PAUL
          It's a plague. And you? You'll be
          here, too?

                    MARY
          All by my lonesome. My little
          sister Peggy and her husband
          invited me to go visit them in
          Roxbury, but I guess I feel like
          it's too soon. Like Curtis will
          think that I'm abandoning him.
          This is the last place my baby and
          I were together, not counting the
          bus station.

Paul wants to comfort her but is ill-equipped.

                    PAUL
          Well, I look forward to your fine
          cooking.

                    MARY
          Oh no. Don't do that. All we've
          got is whatever's left in the walk-
          in. No new deliveries 'til
          January.

He spots a bottle of BOURBON.

                    PAUL
          Mind if I...

                    MARY
          You want some of that? All right.

                    PAUL
          Thank you.

She grabs a mug for him and reaches for the bottle.

                    MARY
                (pouring)
            It's a necessity.

                    PAUL
            Oh yes.

INT. INFIRMARY - DUSK

Their beds staked out, the boys are settling in.

Angus roots through his suitcase. Kountze tosses a tennis
ball against the wall close to Park, who reads a book.

                    ANGUS
            Where's my photo?

                    KOUNTZE
            What photo?

                    ANGUS
            I think you know what photo, and
            you stole it.

                    KOUNTZE
            I resent that baseless accusation.

                    ANGUS
            Give me my goddamn picture!

Kountze leaps to his feet, relishing the confrontation.

                    KOUNTZE
            What's your problem, Tully?
            Homesick? You gonna cry? Little
            boy miss his mommy?

                    ANGUS
            Fuck you, Kountze. Why are you
            even here anyway? Where's your
            family?

                    KOUNTZE
            We're renovating our house. It's
            all torn up. They're storing tools
            and stuff in my room.

                    ANGUS
            That's what they told you? It's
            winter, idiot. Nobody renovates
            their house in the winter.
                (MORE)

                    ANGUS (CONT'D)
Your parents don't want you around
because you're a fucking insecure
sociopath.

                    SMITH
Hey, take it easy, guys.

                    KOUNTZE
A... what?

                    ANGUS
Who'd want you for a son? That's
why you grind everybody, because
deep down you know you're an
asshole - if you even have a deep
down. Plus, academically, you're a
disaster. If I were your parents,
I'd never want you home again. The
only tool in your room is you.

As the enormity and accuracy of this lands on Kountze, he
LUNGES at Angus. Real violence. Smith pulls them apart.

FOOTSTEPS in the hallway. Paul enters and surveys the room.
Kountze is in the corner, wounded and shaken. Angus is
flushed. Their uniforms are askew.

Paul glares, waiting for someone to break.

                    OLLERMAN
They weren't fighting.

                    PAUL
I see. And who started it? The not
fighting. Mr. Tully, perhaps you
could shed some light on the
subject. No? Mr. Kountze? Mr.
Smith? Mr. Ollerman? Mr. Park?
     (off their silence)
All right then, we'll do it like
the Roman Legions. Absent a
confession, one man's sin is every
man's suffering. For every minute
the truth is withheld, you will all
receive a detention.

                    ANGUS
And I thought all the Nazis were
hiding in Argentina.

The boys suppress a laugh.

                    PAUL
          Stifle it, Tully. Now in the first
          of said detentions, you will clean
          the library. Top to bottom.
          Scraping the underside of the
          desks, which are caked with snot
          and gum and all manner of ancient,
          unspeakable proteins. On your
          hands and knees, down in the dust,
          breathing in the dead skin of
          generations of students and
          desiccated cockroach assholes.

                    OLLERMAN
          It was Kountze! Kountze started it!

                    PAUL
          Bravo, Mr. Ollerman. Bravo.

INT. DINING HALL - NIGHT

Kountze sits apart and with no plate.

Mary enters and sets down a platter of chicken, potatoes and
asparagus in front of Paul and the other boys.

                    PAUL
          Lovely. Thank you, Mary.

As Mary returns to the kitchen, the boys reach for the food,
all hands and elbows.

                    SMITH
          Didn't we already have this for
          lunch?

                    KOUNTZE
          And it was crappy then.

                    PAUL
          Consider yourselves lucky. During
          the third Punic campaign, 149-146
          B.C., the Romans laid siege to
          Carthage for three entire years.
          By the time it ended, the
          Carthaginians were reduced to
          eating sand and drinking their own
          urine. Hence the term *punitive*.

Mary returns to the table with a pitcher of water.

PAUL (CONT'D)
Mary, maybe you'd, um, maybe you'd
care to join us.

Kountze looks up -- "Join us?" Mary clocks his disdain.

MARY
I'm all right, thank you.

Mary exits.

KOUNTZE
I mean, I know she's sad about her
son and everything, but still,
she's being paid to do a job. And
she should do it well, right?

The other boys are unsure whether to agree or be horrified,
or both.

KOUNTZE (CONT'D)
But I guess no matter how bad a
cook she is, now they can never
fire her.

PAUL
(slamming his silverware)
Will you shut up! You have no idea
what that woman has...
(reining it in)
For most people, Mr. Kountze, life
is like a henhouse ladder -- shitty
and short. You were born lucky.
Maybe someday you entitled little
degenerates will appreciate that.
If you don't, I feel sorry for you,
and we will not have done our jobs.
Now eat!

INT. INFIRMARY - NIGHT

Paul opens the door, looks inside. The boys are asleep.

INT. BARTON ACADEMY - VARIOUS LOCATIONS - NIGHT

Like a night watchman, Paul, keys and flashlight in hand,
checks the campus -- CLASSROOMS, MUSIC ROOM, BASEMENT. He
opens each door, peers inside. All quiet. Finally, he peers
into the HEADMASTER'S OFFICE. His beam finds the bottle of
Cognac.

INT. BACK STAIRWAY - NIGHT

Climbing stairs, Paul hears TV LAUGHTER.

INT. KITCHEN STAFF COMMON ROOM - CONTINUOUS

Paul follows the sound through an auxiliary kitchen and finds
Mary smoking, shelling walnuts and watching TV, a bottle of
bourbon and a mug nearby.

>   MARY
>   Good evening.

>   PAUL
>   Good evening. What's this?

>   MARY
>   You don't know The Newlywed Game?
>   What planet have you been living
>   on?

>   PAUL
>   I don't really watch television.

>   MARY
>   It's a show where they ask couples
>   questions to see how well they know
>   each other.

>   PAUL
>   That sounds like courting disaster.

>   MARY
>   That's the whole damn point. Sit
>   down. Broaden your horizons.

He sits on the couch. She crosses to the kitchen.

>   MARY (CONT'D)
>   This is a re-run from July, which
>   is why they're playing for the
>   Weber barbecue and picnic utensils.

>   PAUL
>   Fascinating.

Mary returns with a second mug. She sits down next to him
and pours him a shot.

>   PAUL (CONT'D)
>   Thank you.

                    MARY
          Uh-huh. So how are the boys?

                    PAUL
          Broken, in body and spirit.

                    MARY
          It's the holidays. Go easy on
          them.

                    PAUL
          Please. They've had it easy their
          whole lives.

                    MARY
          You don't know that. Did *you*?
          Besides, everybody should be with
          their people on Christmas.

The wind whistles outside, competing with the rise and fall
of TV laughter. Paul sips his bourbon. Mary nods at the TV.

                    MARY (CONT'D)
          Those two are going to get
          divorced.

                    PAUL
          How do you know?

                    MARY
          I recognize that look of stale
          disappointment. She hates him.

                    PAUL
          How long were you married?

                    MARY
          I was engaged to Curtis's father,
          but he died before I gave birth.
               (off Paul's look)
          Harold worked in the shipyards.
          And one day, they were carrying
          this big cargo pallet and the cable
          snapped. Hit him right across the
          head. They were good men, both of
          them, and neither one of them made
          it to twenty-five. My baby wasn't
          even twenty.

                    PAUL
          I'm so sorry.

                    MARY
          I took this job when Curtis was
          little, so he could get a good
          education. You know, he flourished
          here.

                    PAUL
          He was a great kid. I had him one
          semester. Very insightful.

                    MARY
          Uh-huh. He hated you. He said you
          were a real asshole.

                    PAUL
          Well, like I said, sharp kid.
          Insightful.

                    MARY
          He had his heart set on Swarthmore,
          and he had the grades, but I didn't
          have the money. Even with
          financial aid it wasn't enough. So
          when he got called up, no student
          deferment, off he went. You know
          what he said to me? He said: "Hey
          ma, look at the upside. When I get
          discharged, I can go to college on
          the GI Bill." College.
                  (keeping it together)
          And here we are. With my Curtis in
          the cold ground, and those boys
          safe and warm in their beds. It's
          like you said. "Life is like a
          henhouse ladder." That's right --
          I can hear everything you're saying
          from the kitchen. Especially that
          little Kountze kid. Crown prince
          of all the little assholes.

Silence, which is broken by APPLAUSE from the studio
audience.

UNDER BLACK --

                    DAY 4 - DECEMBER 21, 1970

INT. INFIRMARY - MORNING

Paul enters, stares at the sleeping boys, then BANGS BEDPANS.

                    PAUL
          All right, you fetid layabouts.
          It's daylight in the swamp.

The boys groan themselves awake.

                    PAUL (CONT'D)
          Arise!

EXT. QUAD - DAY

The boys run laps as Paul, in his duffle coat, smokes and
motions, "Go faster."

                    PAUL
          Speed! Without sufficient
          exercise, the body devours itself!

Glaring, they pick up the pace. Paul coughs and hacks.

INT. THE "SCHOOL ROOM" - DAY

The boys study inside an immense study hall with 250 desks.
Paul sits reading at the proctor's table.

Angus has an English textbook open, inside of which is an
issue of ZAP comics... and the SKIN MAG he got from Harriman.

Kountze stares at him, seething. Angus smiles and flips him
off.

INT. MARY'S APARTMENT - DAY

It's full of books and family photos, many of Curtis, of
course. Music plays softly on a hi-fi.

Mary sits at her dining table doing a CROSSWORD PUZZLE.

EXT. RIVERBANK - DAY

The boys walk along the river. Church bells echo and die in
the distance.

Smith leads, football in hand. Angus brandishes a branch.

                    ANGUS
          What about your car? We could take
          it. Go somewhere. Boston maybe.

                    SMITH
          Nah, we'd get in so much trouble.
          Face it, man. We're stuck.

Smith stops to spark a joint.

                    ANGUS
          If we just had some way to get out
          of here. Just split.

                    SMITH
          Hell, you could put a chopper down
          right in the Quad.

                    ANGUS
          A what?

                    KOUNTZE
          A helicopter, dumb ass. His old
          man's CEO of Pratt & Whitney.

                    SMITH
          Got his own bird. Takes it from
          Stamford to the city every morning.
          Lands right in our back yard.
          Pilot's name is Wild Bill.

                    PARK
          Wild Bill.

                    SMITH
          Flew up to Haystack with it. Took
          the presents and everything. Minus
          me.

                    OLLERMAN
          Flying with presents, like Santa
          Claus.

                    SMITH
          Yeah. Just like Santa Claus.

Smith glances at Kountze as if to say "go long." Smith tosses
him the football, and they drift away, playing catch.

                    OLLERMAN
          If I was back home right now back
          in Provo, it would be really warm
          inside, and my mom would be making
          baked apples, and the whole house
          would smell like cinnamon and brown
          sugar.

                    PARK
          That sounds so nice.

Kountze runs back into frame, grabs one of Ollerman's gloves
and throws it in the river.

                    OLLERMAN
          Hey!

                    KOUNTZE
          That's what you get for ratting me
          out, little Mormon.

Kountze shoves Ollerman to the ground and, laughing, runs to
catch up with Smith. Ollerman heads over to retrieve his
glove.

                    PARK
          What's Fork Union? Before, you
          said you don't want to end up at
          Fork Union.

                    ANGUS
          It's a military academy in Virginia.
          That's where I'm going if I get
          kicked out of school again.

                    PARK
          How many schools have you been
          kicked out of already?

                    ANGUS
          Three. That's why I'm still a
          junior. Give or take a semester.

Ollerman returns, breathing hard.

                    OLLERMAN
          It's gone! My glove's gone!

                    ANGUS
          Twisted fucker orphaned that glove
          on purpose. Left you with one so
          the loss would sting that much
          more.

Ollerman thinks, then runs back to throw his other glove into
the river. Angus smiles at the sheer poetry of his action.

The glove floats downstream. Ollerman watches it disappear.

INT. INFIRMARY - NIGHT

Angus awakens to Park crying in the bed next to his.

>   ANGUS
>   You all right?

>   PARK
>   I had a nightmare.

Angus sits up and turns to Park.

>   ANGUS
>   I get nightmares, too. I'm always
>   falling. Or drowning.

>   PARK
>   Also, I had an accident.

>   ANGUS
>   (feeling)
>   Yeah, you did. Shhh. Stop crying.
>   If they hear, they'll crucify you.
>   Which would be ironic, since you're
>   Buddhist.

>   PARK
>   I know it's an excellent school,
>   and my brothers went here. But I
>   miss my family, and I have no
>   friends.

>   ANGUS
>   Yeah, well, friends are overrated.
>   I'll help you hide the sheets in
>   the morning, all right? In the
>   meantime, find a dry spot, and try
>   to get some sleep.

>   PARK
>   Thank you.

Park smiles, consoled. Angus lies down. Sniffs his hand.

>   ANGUS
>   Fucking asparagus.

UNDER BLACK --

DAY 5 - DECEMBER 22, 1970

INT. FOUNDERS' ROOM LIBRARY - DAY

The boys study. Paul reads, mug at his elbow, and coughs
wetly.

> SMITH
> (whispering)
> You kidding me? It's only eleven
> and he's already lit. I can smell
> the whiskey on him.

> ANGUS
> Can you blame him? It's freezing in
> here. It's fucking Greenland in
> here.

All notice the sound of a faint ROAR growing in volume.

> PAUL
> What the hell is that?

Paul and the boys rush to the window to see --

A HELICOPTER ABOUT TO LAND

INT. KITCHEN - CONTINUOUS

Also hearing the noise, Mary approaches the window.

INT. FOUNDERS' ROOM LIBRARY - CONTINUOUS

Paul and the boys watch the chopper touch down near the Quad.
Out steps handsome captain of industry HARRY "SKIP" SMITH.

> SMITH
> He finally caved, the big softie.
> (racing to the door)
> Hey, any of you guys like to ski?

Smith runs to greet his dad. The boys look at each other
hopefully.

INT. ADMINISTRATIVE OFFICE HALLWAY - DAY

The boys peer through the office window as Paul speaks on the
phone and Jason Smith chats amiably with his father.

Paul hangs up and turns to the Smiths. Jason grins and
flashes a THUMBS-UP to his friends in the hallway.

                    KOUNTZE
          Yes!

                    PAUL
              (opening the door)
          Gentlemen, good news. I was able
          to reach Dr. Woodrup and your
          parents. Most of them, anyway.

Paul glances at Angus. His face falls.

INT. ADMINISTRATIVE OFFICE HALLWAY - DAY

Angus pleads with Paul.

                    ANGUS
          Try calling again. Just one more
          time. Please.

                    PAUL
          There's no point. The desk clerk
          said no one's answering. He says
          they're away on some excursion.

                    ANGUS
          Excursion.

                    PAUL
          I'm as disappointed as you are, if
          not more so. I could be spending
          the rest of my vacation reading
          mystery novels.

                    ANGUS
          Maybe they're back by now. Just
          call again.

                    PAUL
          Okay.

INT. INFIRMARY - DAY

CLOSE ON ANGUS, as the other boys merrily pack up their
suitcases. Park hauls his bag off the bed and heads toward
the door, his sad eyes burning with survivor's guilt.

                    PARK
          Happy Holidays.

                    ANGUS
          Same to you.

Park leaves. Smith emerges.

> SMITH
> Take care, Tully.

Smith follows Park. Now Kountze passes Angus, suitcase in hand.

> KOUNTZE
> Guess that just leaves you, huh? Be sure to get all your homework done. Oh, I almost forgot. I found that picture you were looking for.

Kountze tucks a photo into Angus's shirt pocket.

> KOUNTZE (CONT'D)
> Merry Christmas, Mr. Tully.

Kountze exits. Angus pulls the picture out -- it's him at eleven on a beach smiling with his mom and dad. Across their faces is scrawled the word "fuckwad." Ollerman walks past with his bag, smiling that cinnamon-and-brown sugar smile.

> OLLERMAN
> Bye, Angus!

EXT. QUAD - DAY

The helicopter flies away. Observing, Paul and Angus turn grimly to each other. Hard to tell who's more disappointed.

> PAUL
> Let's try to make the best of it, shall we?

Paul hesitantly pats his shoulder. Percolating with hurt and rage, Angus just stares at the empty horizon.

INT. KITCHEN STAFF COMMON ROOM - NIGHT

Paul and Mary watch "The Newlywed Game" and drink from mugs. Angus is there as well, flopped on a sofa, half watching, half paging through a magazine.

> MARY
> How about you? You ever been married?

Paul shakes his head, grimacing at the notion.

                    PAUL
          No. I did get close. Once. Right
          after college.

                    MARY
          And?

                    PAUL
          We came to our senses.
               (pointing)
          This is not exactly a face forged
          for romance.

Mary looks at him -- the pipe, the scowl, the wonky eye.
Angus glances over, too.

                    MARY
               (gesturing to his armpits)
          And, the uh... you know...

                    PAUL
          What?

                    MARY
          Nothing.

                    PAUL
          I don't know. I like being alone.
          Always found myself drawn to the
          ascetic. Like a monk. The
          foregoing of sensual pleasure for
          the achievement of spiritual goals.

                    MARY
          Spiritual goals? You? What kind
          of spiritual goals are you talking
          about? You go to church?

                    PAUL
          Only when required.

                    MARY
          When's the last time you even left
          campus?

                    PAUL
          I go into town all the time. For
          groceries and various errands and
          appointments.
               (of her look)
          OK, yes. I don't leave campus
          often. Don't really feel the need.

>   MARY
>   Let me ask you something: if you
>   could go anywhere on Earth, where
>   would you go?

>   PAUL
>   Oh... Greece, Italy, Egypt, Peru.
>   Carthage -- Tunisia now, of course.
>   In college I started a monograph on
>   Carthage. I'd like to finish it
>   one day. A monograph is like a
>   book, only shorter.

>   MARY
>   I know what a monograph is.

>   ANGUS
>   Why not just write a book?

>   PAUL
>   I'm not sure I have an entire book
>   in me.

Mary and Angus exchange a look.

>   MARY
>   You can't even have a whole dream,
>   can you?

INT. NURSE'S QUARTERS - NIGHT

Paul, now in pajamas, occupies this separate, spartan space --
a bed and a sink -- used occasionally by a nurse. He
stretches unsteadily, picks up a nearby bottle of Jim Beam
and takes a deep pull. He puts the bottle down, mutters to
himself and collapses heavily onto the thin mattress.

INT. NURSE'S QUARTERS - LATER

Paul is passed out atop the covers. The door opens. Angus
peers inside, enters quietly, and glances around the room.

He sees the RING OF KEYS and the FLASHLIGHT.

INT. KITCHEN - NIGHT

Angus raids the freezer and chips away at a tub of freezer-
burned ice cream.

INT. CHAPEL - SACRISTY - NIGHT

Angus pours sacramental wine into a chalice. Gulps it down.
Not bad! Hits it again.

INT. KITCHEN STAFF COMMON ROOM - NIGHT

Angus peers at Mary, asleep on the couch, test pattern on the
TV.

INT. CHAPEL - NIGHT

Angus sits at the piano. Lights a cigarette. Strikes one
key. As the note decays, he expels a column of smoke that
hangs in the moonlight.

INT. CHAPEL - DAWN

Angus sits in the front pew, contemplating the photo of
Curtis Lamb by the altar.

Mary enters the chapel, takes off her winter coat and takes a
seat in a rear pew.

Angus notices her and nods a greeting. She nods back.

UNDER BLACK --
                    DAY 6 - DECEMBER 23, 1970

INT. DINING HALL - DAY

Paul and Angus eat lunch. Mary has coffee and a smoke.

                    PAUL
          I have a surprise.

He produces the Christmas cookies Miss Crane gave him.

                    PAUL (CONT'D)
          These were a gift to me, and I
          would like to share them with both
          of you. Look at them. Look at the
          festive shapes. Snowflakes.
          Gingerbread men. A tree. A little
          mitten. And they've got frosting!

Paul smiles thinly, bites into one, makes "yummy" noises.
Angus stares at this loser.

                    ANGUS
          May I go to the bathroom, sir?

                    PAUL
          You may.

Angus stalks out of the room. Paul looks at Mary, flummoxed.

                    PAUL (CONT'D)
          Well, I'm trying.

Mary can't help but laugh at his pathetic attempt.

INT. HALLWAY - DAY

Angus talks on a PAY PHONE.

                    ANGUS
          Well, if you don't have a single
          room, I'll take a junior suite or
          the equivalent. I fully understand
          it's the holidays, but it's kind of
          an emergency.

Paul comes around the corner.

                    PAUL
          Mr. Tully, what are you doing?

                    ANGUS
              (holding up a finger)
          No, no credit card. I'll pay cash
          or traveler's checks.

                    PAUL
          I didn't say you could use the
          phone.

                    ANGUS
          I see. Okay, then can you
          recommend somewhere else, maybe
          downtown?

Paul hangs up the phone on him.

                    PAUL
          Was that a hotel?

                    ANGUS
          None of your business.

                    PAUL
          It is absolutely my business. I'm
          looking after you.

                    ANGUS
          Looking after me? Like what, like
          my warden? Like my butler?
          There's nobody here, okay? Just us
          two losers and a grieving mom, so
          let's cut the shit. You stay out
          of my way, and I'll stay out of
          yours.

Paul stares at him incredulously, then pulls a slip of paper
from his pocket.

                    PAUL
          That's a detention.

Angus walks away.

                    PAUL (CONT'D)
          You just earned a detention, sir.
          Now get back here.

                    ANGUS
          Being here with you is already one
          big fucking detention!

                    PAUL
          Son of a *bitch*. That's another
          detention!

Angus sets off down the hallway, knocking over trash cans,
tearing down fliers, general mayhem. Paul chases him.

                    PAUL (CONT'D)
          I don't know what you're playing
          at, Mr. Tully, but you are courting
          disaster.

Angus rounds a corner, stops, and turns to peer back at Paul,
who is huffing and puffing in pursuit.

                    ANGUS
          Without sufficient exercise, the
          body devours itself.

As Paul struggles to catch up, Angus sprints away.

                    PAUL
          You are careening toward a
          suspension!

INT. TROPHY ROOM - DAY

Angus dashes up stairs and across a room filled with
mementoes honoring past athletes. He stops to wait for Paul,
who is out of breath on the steps.

Once Paul reaches the top, Angus cartwheels toward the door
to the --

INT. NEW GYMNASIUM - CONTINUOUS

Angus stands at the threshold. It's pristine. Jordan
Osgood's father really did spend a lot.

> PAUL
> Don't even think about it, Mr.
> Tully!
> (catching up)
> You are a hair's breadth from
> suspension. I'll wash my hands of
> you. You hear me? Wash my hands.
> Stop right there. You know the gym
> is strictly off limits. This is
> your Rubicon. Do not cross the
> Rubicon.

Angus steps onto the freshly lacquered floor.

> ANGUS
> *Alea jacta est.*

Despite the circumstances, Paul is impressed by Angus's
reference.

Angus eyes a POMMEL HORSE across the gym, takes a deep breath
and runs toward it. He vaults over it but topples clumsily --
and hard -- on the other side.

A beat, then Angus rises to his knees, his LEFT ARM DANGLING
oddly. He SCREAMS in agony.

> ANGUS (CONT'D)
> Oh fuck! Mr. Hunham!

Paul goes white.

EXT. FACULTY PARKING LOT - DAY

A frantic Paul struggles to scrape the windshield of his 1964
NOVA. In excruciating pain, Angus wears his coat with only
one arm in a sleeve.

                    ANGUS
          Hurry up! Hurry!

                    PAUL
          I *am* hurrying!

INT. NOVA - DAY

Paul white-knuckles the wheel. Angus whimpers in the back.

                    PAUL
          I was on thin ice already. If
          Woodrup finds out, the facts won't
          matter. He'll make it my fault.

                    ANGUS
          It is your fault.

                    PAUL
          What?

                    ANGUS
          You said it yourself. You were
          supposed to be looking after me.

                    PAUL
          I told you to stop!

                    ANGUS
          You said you washed your hands of
          me.

                    PAUL
          I meant it metaphorically.

                    ANGUS
          Of course you meant it
          metaphorically. What were you
          going to do, actually go and wash
          your hands?!

Angus chokes back tears, the effort transforming his face.
Paul realizes he's just a terrified kid with a fucked-up arm.

INT. BARTON HOSPITAL - EMERGENCY ROOM - DAY

Angus and Paul sit in a hallway.

                    PAUL
          This is the end. They'll inform
          the school, who will inform your
          parents, and then it's curtains.
          You're going to get me fired. You!

                    ANGUS
          I'm the one who might lose an arm,
          and all you can think about is
          yourself.

A friendly NURSE comes by and hands Paul a clipboard.

                    NURSE
          If you could just fill this out,
          please. Admissions and insurance.

Paul reluctantly starts writing -- it's going to be official
now. Angus clocks Paul's dread and calls the Nurse back.

                    ANGUS
          Excuse me. Is there any way we
          could skip this whole insurance
          thing?

                    NURSE
          It's just standard procedure.

                    ANGUS
          I understand. But look, we were
          over at Squantz pond playing
          hockey, and I slipped on the ice.

                    PAUL
          Angus, what are you doing?

                    ANGUS
          My mom told him not to take me, but
          I made him. My folks are divorced,
          and we don't get to see each other
          very often. She'll be mad as a
          hornet if she finds out.

                    NURSE
          Okay, that's your business. But we
          just have certain protocols.

                    PAUL
          Yeah. Protocols.

                    ANGUS
          Please. I never get to see my dad.
          It was my fault, all mine. I don't
          want to get him in trouble.
                    (MORE)

ANGUS (CONT'D)
(to Paul)
I don't want her dragging you to
court again.
(to the Nurse)
Can we can skip the whole insurance
thing? We can pay cash. Right,
Dad?

INT. BARTON HOSPITAL - TREATMENT ROOM - LATER

A shirtless Angus sits on a stretcher, his shoulder blade
protruding at a sickening angle. Paul stands nearby. A
young INTERN points at an x-ray.

INTERN
The good news is nothing's broken.

PAUL
Thank God.

INTERN
But you did dislocate your shoulder
pretty badly.

ANGUS
What does that mean?

INTERN
That means your arm has popped out
of the socket, and we just have to
pop it back in.

ANGUS
Is it going to hurt?

INTERN
Not if you relax. The key is to
relax. Deep breaths.

The Intern and the Nurse wind a bedsheet around Angus,
creating a slipknot with Angus's shoulder at the center.

INTERN (CONT'D)
On three. One, two, three.

The Intern and the Nurse yank the bedsheet in opposite
directions. Angus writhes and SCREAMS.

We hold on Paul's horrified face and hear a wet POP!

PAUL
Jesus!

INT. BARTON HOSPITAL - PHARMACY - DAY

His arm now in a SLING, Angus walks with Paul toward a small dispensary.

> PAUL
> Barton men don't do that.

> ANGUS
> Do what?

> PAUL
> Barton men don't lie.

> ANGUS
> Yeah, well, I had momentum.

Paul hands over a prescription to a PHARMACIST.

> PAUL
> Hello, we have this, uh...

> PHARMACIST
> Percodan, huh? Okay, give me a few minutes.

The Pharmacist walks away.

> ANGUS
> You said that if Woodrup finds out, you're screwed. So now he won't find out.

> PAUL
> What happens if your parents inquire?

> ANGUS
> Never going to happen. Trust me.

> PAUL
> Okay, then. This all remains *entre nous*. Got it? You know what *entre nous* means?

> ANGUS
> *Oui, monsieur.* Now you owe me.

> PAUL
> Owe you? Do not try to leverage me, Mr. Tully.

                    ANGUS
          All I'm looking for is little thank
          you that I did something nice for
          you. That's all.

EXT. THE WINNING TICKET - EVENING

A weather-beaten watering hole in the heart of Barton.

INT. THE WINNING TICKET - EVENING

A working class tavern -- pizza, burgers, beer, jukebox,
pinball machines. A TV shows protests, Nixon, and choppers
with wounded.

Paul and Angus sit at a table. Angus scans the menu.

                    ANGUS
          I think I'll start with a beer.
          How about you?

                    PAUL
          Don't be ridiculous, Mr. Tully.

                    ANGUS
          We've had a hard day. We deserve
          to loosen up a little.

                    PAUL
          You've had ten milligrams of
          Percodan. You're plenty loose
          already.

                    ANGUS
          They've got Miller High Life.
          "The Champagne of Beers."

A WAITRESS approaches. Why, it's none other than --

                    PAUL
          Miss Crane. As I live and breathe.
          What are you doing here?

                    MISS CRANE
          Hi, guys. Yeah, I always pick up a
          little extra work over Thanksgiving
          and Christmas.

                    PAUL
          This is Mr. Tully.

                    MISS CRANE
          Sure, I know you.

                    ANGUS
          Angus Tully. We met outside Dr.
          Woodrup's office. I was wrongly
          accused of blowing up a toilet.

                    MISS CRANE
          I didn't know about the "wrongly"
          part.

                    PAUL
          He'll have a cheeseburger.

                    ANGUS
          And a Miller High Life, please.

                    PAUL
          No, you will not.

                    ANGUS
          Where do you stand on Miller High
          Life, Miss Crane? Quality-wise.

                    MISS CRANE
          Well, like they say, it's the
          Champagne of Beers.

                    ANGUS
          And she's a professional.

                    MISS CRANE
          Okay, well, one cheeseburger.

                    ANGUS
               (reluctantly)
          And a Coke.

                    PAUL
               (to Miss Crane)
          I'll have a cheeseburger as well.

                    MISS CRANE
          Two cheeseburgers.

                    PAUL
          And a Jim Beam. On the rocks.
          Please.

She smiles and exits. Paul watches her go. Angus grins.

                    ANGUS
          Ouch. You two have chemistry.

                    PAUL
          That's the Percodan talking.

                    ANGUS
          Seeing her like this, I think she's
          pretty attractive.

                    PAUL
          Listen, you hormonal vulgarian,
          that woman deserves your respect,
          not your erotic speculation.

                    ANGUS
          May I at least go to the bathroom?
          Sir?

                    PAUL
          You mean the payphone.

They stare at each other. Angus peels off to the bathroom.
Miss Crane returns.

                    MISS CRANE
          A Coke and a double Jim. I charged
          you for a single.

                    PAUL
          Thank you. Chin chin.

                    MISS CRANE
          So how'd you get stuck holding
          over? I thought this was Mr.
          Endicott's year.

                    PAUL
          I'm being punished. Dr. Woodrup
          is, how can I put this --

                    MISS CRANE
          A pompous ass with a dictator
          complex? Oops. What I meant to
          say was that he's a lovely,
          compassionate educator with really
          groovy beard.

                    PAUL
          I've had a lot of former students
          rise to positions of authority, but
          he's the only one I've ever had to
          report to.

                    MISS CRANE
          He was your student?

>   PAUL
> My first year teaching, and he was
> an asshole even then.

Miss Crane LAUGHS. Paul joins in.

>   MISS CRANE
> Well, listen, if you and Angus are
> really all alone up there, I'm
> having a little Christmas Eve
> party, in case, you know, you guys
> want to stop by.

Miss Crane smiles warmly. Paul smiles back, a deer in the
headlights.

OUTSIDE THE MEN'S ROOM

Angus exits and sees a young man playing pinball, kind of a
PINBALL WIZARD. Angus approaches and lays a COIN on the edge
of the machine.

>   PINBALL WIZARD
> Sorry, kid. Next game's taken.

>   ANGUS
> But I just put a dime down.

>   PINBALL WIZARD
> Don't care. My buddy's up next.

>   ANGUS
> That's not how it works.

>   PINBALL WIZARD
> That's how it works in here. Why
> don't you go shoot the other
> fuckin' machine.

>   ANGUS
> Because I don't want to shoot the
> other fuckin' machine.

Angus stares at him. He breaks his focus and loses the game.

>   PINBALL WIZARD
> Thanks for fuckin' up my mojo.
> Kenny! You're up.

>   ANGUS
> Bullshit. I put my dime down, so
> I'm up next.

                         VOICE (O.C.)
              What was that?

Angus turns to see KENNETH, a YOUNG VET in an army jacket, a
little drunk, and a HOOK where his right hand should be.

                         ANGUS
              Oh.

Angus stares at the hook.

                         KENNETH
              Hey, sport, my eyes are up here.

                         PINBALL WIZARD
              Look at this kid. Spoiled little
              Barton boy.

                         KENNETH
              Yeah, he's a fancy little prick,
              isn't he?

                         ANGUS
              It's fine. You can take my dime.

                         KENNETH
              Take it? You want me to take your
              dime? Like it's charity?

                         ANGUS
              No, what I meant is we can play
              together. You can be my left arm.

                         KENNETH
              What the fuck did you just say to
              me?

Kenneth steps toward Angus. They're nearly nose to nose now.

AT THE TABLE

Paul chats with Miss Crane. Angus run/walks up the two of
them with Kenneth and the Pinball Wizard in hot pursuit.

                         ANGUS
              Mr. Hunham, can we go, please?

                         PAUL
              Why?

                         ANGUS
              I've been called a fancy little
              prick. We should go.

                    KENNETH
                (approaching)
          Hey, why'd you run off? We were
          talking to you. Don't they teach
          you manners at that school?

Kenneth pokes Angus in the chest with his hook.

                    MISS CRANE
          No, no, no. Kenneth, leave him
          alone. They just came in for some
          food.

Kenneth closes on Angus. Mayhem is a moment away.

                    PAUL
          Kenneth, is that right? I don't
          doubt that he did something to
          offend you. It's his specialty.
          Perhaps I could purchase you
          gentlemen something to imbibe, and
          we could let whatever this
          unfortunate incident is go the way
          of the dodo.

                    PINBALL WIZARD
          The what?⬜⬜

                    ANGUS
          The dodo. It's an extinct bird.

                    MISS CRANE
          What he's saying is he wants to buy
          you guys a beer.

Kenneth considers the offer. Finally, he steps back.

                    KENNETH
          Yeah, okay.

                    PINBALL WIZARD
          Same here. I'll have a Miller.

                    ANGUS
          Champagne of beers!

EXT. BARTON STREET - NIGHT

Paul and Angus leave the tavern.

                    ANGUS
          Why'd you buy those guys beer?
          They're assholes.

                    PAUL
          That's one way to look at it.
          Here, catch.

Paul tosses his keys at Angus, who reflexively catches them.

                    PAUL (CONT'D)
          How many boys do you know who have
          had their hands blown off? Barton
          boys don't go to Vietnam. They go
          to Yale or Dartmouth or Cornell,
          whether they deserve to or not.

                    ANGUS
          Except for Curtis Lamb.

                    PAUL
          Except for Curtis Lamb.

                    ANGUS
          Were you ever in the military?

                    PAUL
          I tried to enlist in '41, but was
          rejected.
               (points to his eyes)
          They made me an air raid warden.
          Gave me a whistle and everything.
          Helmet. Arm band.

EXT. BARTON STREET - MOMENTS LATER

Paul unlocks his Nova, but the door sticks, so he walks
around to unlock the passenger side. He gets inside and
slides over to the driver's seat -- clearly a routine.

                    ANGUS
          Before we get going, can I be
          candid with you? You smell.

INT. NOVA - CONTINUOUS

Angus gets in the car, too. Paul looks at him sadly.

                    ANGUS
          Like fish. And it's really
          noticeable toward the end of the
          day. I even smell it on your coat.
          Mind if I crack the window?

                    PAUL
          Trimethylaminuria.

                    ANGUS
Huh?

                    PAUL
Trimethylaminuria. It means my body
can't break down trimethylamine.
That's the smell. And yes, more
toward the end of the day.

                    ANGUS
Wow. Your whole life?
    (off Paul's nod)
No wonder you're afraid of women.

                    PAUL
    (stung)
I am not afraid of women. Jesus.

                    ANGUS
I shouldn't have said anything.
Dr. Gertler says I should give more
consideration to my audience.

                    PAUL
Who's Dr. Gertler?

                    ANGUS
My shrink. We're working on it.
And other things.

                    PAUL
Has Dr. Gertler ever tried a swift
kick in the ass?

                    ANGUS
Now your turn. Go ahead, tell me
something about me. Something
negative.

                    PAUL
Something negative about you?

                    ANGUS
Sure. Just one thing.

                    PAUL
Just one?

Angus nods. Paul shoots looks at him, thinking. There are a
hundred things to say, but he just starts the car.

UNDER BLACK --
                    DAY 7 - CHRISTMAS EVE, 1970

INT. DINING HALL - MORNING

Paul and Angus eat breakfast. Mary enters with her coffee.

>   MARY
>   So why'd you two miss supper last
>   night?

>   PAUL
>   We went into town on some school-
>   related business.

>   MARY
>   You could have called.

>   PAUL
>   Sorry.

Danny -- the custodian with the snowblower from the opening --
enters, carrying a mop and bucket.

>   DANNY
>   Good morning, everybody.

>   PAUL
>   Hi, Danny.

>   MARY
>   Go on in. Make yourself a plate.

>   DANNY
>   I just saw something funny. I
>   walked into the gym and somebody
>   had vomited in there.

Mary raises an eyebrow at Paul and Angus.

>   PAUL
>   You don't say. I don't know
>   anything about that.

>   ANGUS
>   Me neither.

>   PAUL
>   I'll look into that right away.
>   Thank you.

>   MARY
>   Mm-hmm. I see how it is.

She looks at Danny. Danny sets the mop and bucket down
beside Angus, then heads into the kitchen. Mary lights a
cigarette and follows.

EXT. QUAD - DAY

Taking a vigorous "constitutional," Paul finds a FOOTBALL
abandoned in the snow. He stares at it, then picks it up and
throws it. It's the most awkward throw ever.

INT. KITCHEN - DAY

Mary prepares a roast. Paul peels potatoes. A bottle of
bourbon and two mugs sit nearby.

              MARY
I appreciate you pitching in.

              PAUL
No, no. I should be thanking you.
This is very... therapeutic.

              MARY
Try it when you're stuck serving
three hundred little shits who do
nothing but complain, then see how
"therapeutic" it is.

Angus enters and notices a PLATE OF BROWNIES on the table.

              MARY (CONT'D)
Speaking of.

              ANGUS
Brownies? God, yes. I want all of
these.

              MARY
Just take one. The rest are for
the Christmas party tonight.

Angus snags a brownie and devours it.

              ANGUS
           (mouth full)
What Christmas party? There's a
Christmas party?

              MARY
At Miss Crane's house. I'm only
gonna go for a little bit and show
my face. She said she invited you.

              ANGUS
I want to go to the party.

                    PAUL
          She didn't mean it. We were just
          making small talk.

                    MARY
          If you don't want to go, then don't
          go. I'll take him.

                    ANGUS
          Mary can take me.

                    PAUL
          No, that's not how it works.
          You're under my supervision.

                    ANGUS
          Okay, maybe it's fine for you to sit
          around reading books all day, but I
          am losing my goddamned mind! Jesus!

Angus flings his half-finished brownie and storms out.

                    MARY
          Hey! Watch your mouth, young man.
          Not on Christmas!

                    PAUL
          You see? I can't trust him in a
          social situation.

                    MARY
          Mr. Hunham, if you're too
          chickenshit to go to that party,
          then just say so. But don't fuck
          it up for the little asshole!
          What's wrong with you? It's just a
          party. What are you afraid of?

                    PAUL
               (almost inaudibly)
          I don't know.

                    MARY
          Shit. Now you've got me nervous.

INT. INFIRMARY - NIGHT

At a small sink with tiny mirror, Angus tries his hand at
shaving. Really, there's no need.

INT. MARY'S APARTMENT - NIGHT

In a robe, Mary stands in front of her open closet flipping through dresses.

CURTIS'S DRESS UNIFORM hangs among her clothes. She pauses when she comes to it, then looks at a worn BROWN CARDBOARD BOX on the shelf above it. She touches the box, then chooses an outfit.

She glances out the window. It's SNOWING again.

INT. NURSE'S QUARTERS - NIGHT

Paul stands at a mirror in a fresh shirt and tie under his corduroy jacket. He smooths his hair, checks his breath, discreetly smells himself. Not good. He heads into --

THE BATHROOM

-- where he finds a can of AIR FRESHENER, sprays a little under each arm of his jacket. Sniffs. Close enough.

EXT. NEW ENGLAND ROAD - NIGHT

The Nova rattles past shuttered shops and darkened homes strung with Christmas lights.

EXT. MISS CRANE'S HOUSE - NIGHT

A modest house on a tree-lined street.

Paul, Mary and Angus stand on the porch. Miss Crane opens the door. Already a little lit, she wears a bright "midi" dress and holds a highball.

                    MISS CRANE
          You made it! I'm so glad you're
          here.

                    MARY
          We're happy to be here.
               (lifting the foil)
          Where should I put these?

                    MISS CRANE
          Your brownies. Those you can put
          on my bedside table.

                    MARY
          You are a wicked woman.

                    MISS CRANE
          Oh, you have no idea.

They share a laugh. Miss Crane takes Mary's arm and leads her
into the party. Paul and Angus follow.

INT. MISS CRANE'S HOUSE - LIVING ROOM - NIGHT

A Christmas party is in full swing. There's a large silver
Christmas tree in the corner. ADULTS drink, talk, laugh,
smoke. KIDS run around.

                    PAUL
          Certainly a lot of people here.

                    MISS CRANE
          It's mostly family, some friends
          from town. Only you guys from
          work. That's my mom over there.

She points to an OLDER LADY on the sofa, chatting with
friends.

Then she points at a PRETTY WOMAN holding a THREE-YEAR-OLD
BOY. The boy wears a dress shirt, tie and shoes, but no
pants.

                    MISS CRANE (CONT'D)
          That's my sister Kathy and her son
          Marvin.

She points to ANOTHER MAN standing with a twelve-year-old
BOY, both in matching turtlenecks.

                    MISS CRANE (CONT'D)
          That's my friend Tom -- he owns the
          men's clothing store on Bellamy
          Street -- and his son Brad.

On a mantel crowded with Christmas tchotchkes, Angus spots a
SNOW GLOBE. He picks it up and shakes it. For a moment, the
party falls away completely as he stares at the swirling
snow, lost in a sweet, distant memory.

                    MISS CRANE (CONT'D)
          Angus.

Jolted back to reality, he turns to Miss Crane, who stands
with a lovely GIRL, 16.

                    MISS CRANE (CONT'D)
          This is Angus Tully. He's one of
          our students at Barton. Angus,
          this is my niece, Elise.

                    ANGUS
          Niece Elise. Nice.

Paul gives him a look.

                    MISS CRANE
          This is Mr. Hunham. He's one of
          our finest teachers. History,
          right?

                    PAUL
          Ancient Civilizations, yes.

                    MISS CRANE
          And this is Mary Lamb. She's the
          manager of the cafeteria

                    ELISE
          Hi.

                    MISS CRANE
          Why don't you take Angus to the
          basement and introduce him to our
          family tradition?

Elise leads Angus away.

                    MISS CRANE (CONT'D)
          Let me get you guys some drinks.
          Jim Beam for you, right?

                    PAUL
          Correct.

                    MARY
          I'll take a whiskey.

Miss Crane smiles and wanders off. Paul ambles over to the
buffet. A PARTY GOER smiles at him. Paul smiles back but
makes no effort to engage.

INT. MISS CRANE'S HOUSE - BASEMENT - NIGHT

Elise leads Angus downstairs to sort of ARTSY-CRAFTSY AREA,
where YOUNGER KIDS are gluing Popsicle sticks together and
decorating them with glitter, pipe-cleaners and paint.

Angus can't stop glancing at Elise.

                    ANGUS
          This is what you wanted to show me?

                    ELISE
          I grew up playing down here during
          my aunt's parties. I think it's
          kind of cool. There's a purity to
          it. I mean, every child is an
          artist. The problem is remaining
          an artist when we grow up. Picasso
          said that.

                    ANGUS
          Picasso's cool. I saw *Guérnica*
          once. You know, the big mural,
          with the horse.

He pulls a twisted *Guernica* face.

                    ELISE
          I know *Guérnica*. You really saw
          it?

                    ANGUS
          At the Museum of Modern Art in New
          York. It's huge. My dad took me.

                    ELISE
          Hey, Guernica: you're giving me an
          idea.

INT. MISS CRANE'S HOUSE - DEN - NIGHT

Mary stands by the hi-fi, drink in hand, clearly melancholy.
Custodian Danny enters the party and spots her.

                    DANNY
          There you go. How're you doing
          tonight?

They exchange a chaste little hug.

                    MARY
          I'm doing all right. They put me
          in charge of the music.

                    DANNY
          Who put you in charge of the music?

                    MARY
          I did.

                    DANNY
               (sweetly)
          You're so crazy.

An awkward moment. Danny produces a small gift.

                    DANNY (CONT'D)
          I got you a little something.

                    MARY
          No.

Danny nods -- Go on, open it.

                    MARY (CONT'D)
          Danny, you didn't have to do this.

                    DANNY
          I don't have to do anything except
          pay taxes and die. I wanted to.

She unwraps the gift -- it's a pin.

                    MARY
          This is lovely. Thank you.

                    DANNY
          You're welcome.

                    MARY
          But Danny, I didn't get you
          anything.

                    DANNY
          Yeah, you did. That beautiful
          smile.

Mary smiles, almost despite herself.

                    DANNY (CONT'D)
          There it is.

                    MARY
          Well, then. Merry Christmas.

INT. MISS CRANE'S HOUSE - BASEMENT - NIGHT

Elise and Angus finger-paint.

                    ANGUS
          Am I doing this right?

                    ELISE
          There is no right or wrong.

She leans toward him, spreading the paint across the paper.
Angus tries not to stare.

                    ELISE (CONT'D)
          Are you trying to look down my
          shirt?

                    ANGUS
          No. Yes.

She smiles and keeps on painting.

                    ELISE
          You know, I'm not going to do this
          if you're not going to take it
          seriously.

                    ANGUS
          I am taking it seriously. As
          seriously as one can take finger
          painting.

                    ELISE
          No, you're not. You missed this
          whole area, right here.

She leans closer, pointing to a blank space. Their eyes
meet. She smiles and kisses him gently. We can tell it's
his first. It takes a moment for him to process it before
kissing back.

INT. MISS CRANE'S HOUSE - LIVING ROOM - NIGHT

Paul examines the silver Christmas tree. Miss Crane
approaches with his drink and kisses him on the cheek.

                    PAUL
               (shocked)
          Oh!

She hands him his glass of Jim and points at the ceIling.

                    MISS CRANE
          Mistletoe.

                    PAUL
          Right. Of course.
               (a beat, then, awkwardly)
          You know, it's interesting.
               (MORE)

                        PAUL (CONT'D)
Aeneas carried mistletoe when he
descended into Hades in search of
his father.

                        MISS CRANE
Huh.

                        PAUL
Anyway, I like your tree. Very
space age.

                        MISS CRANE
I bought it to commemorate the moon
landing!

                        PAUL
Really. Oh.

                        MISS CRANE
So where's your family this
Christmas?

                        PAUL
Nowhere. I'm an only child. My
mother died when I was young.

                        MISS CRANE
And your father?

Paul shakes his head, loath to get into something unpleasant.

                        PAUL
Let's just say I left home when I
was fifteen.

                        MISS CRANE
You ran away?

                        PAUL
Worse. I got a scholarship. To
Barton. And from there, I went to
college and never looked back.

                        MISS CRANE
But you did a little. I mean, you came
back here.

Paul looks at her, wheels turning.

                        PAUL
It kind of feels like home. And I
guess I thought I could make a
difference.

                    MISS CRANE
          And do you? Make a difference?

                    PAUL
          I mean, I used to think I could
          prepare them for the world, even a
          little -- provide standards and
          grounding, like Dr. Green always
          drilled into us. But the world
          doesn't make sense anymore. It's
          on fire, the rich don't give a
          shit, poor kids are cannon fodder,
          integrity's a punch line, trust is
          just a name on a bank.

Miss Crane absorbs this and studies Paul.

                    MISS CRANE
          Well, look. If that's all true,
          then now is when they most need
          someone like you.

She smiles at him -- dazzling even with the dark sentiments.
A bittersweet Christmas moment.

BY THE STEREO

Still with Danny and a little drunk, Mary cues up a record,
but she has trouble dropping the needle and makes horrible
scratching noise.

Finally Artie Shaw's "WHEN WINTER COMES" comes on.

                    MARY
          Danny, do you know Curtis used to
          love Artie Shaw? We used to dance
          to this. I mean, what teenage kid
          listens to Artie Shaw?

A MALE GUEST heads toward the stereo.

                    MALE GUEST
          You're kidding me. Can't we play
          something a little hipper?

                    MARY
          Don't touch that goddamn record.

                    DANNY
          Maybe you better sit down.

                    MARY
          Danny, I'm okay.

He puts his arm around her. She removes it.

>   MARY (CONT'D)
>   I said I'm okay!

Teetering, she finds a seat. We move CLOSER to her as she
listens. Danny looks at her, seeing she's unreachable.

>   MARY (CONT'D)
>   Get me another drink.

ON THE COUCH

Miss Crane and Paul are deep into their drinks.

>   MISS CRANE
>   Are you planning anything special
>   for tomorrow?

>   PAUL
>   Why, are you having a...

>   MISS CRANE
>   No, I just thought maybe you'd be
>   doing something special for Angus.
>   (off Paul's head shake)
>   You should. To help preserve some
>   of the magic. He may be a little
>   difficult, but he's still just a
>   kid. And life catches up to them
>   so fast. Them. Ha. Us!

She has a point. Paul looks at her, touched.

>   PAUL
>   You're a very sweet person,
>   Miss Crane.

>   MISS CRANE
>   So are you, when you want to be.
>   And it's Lydia.

He basks in this small intimacy. Behind him, the front door
swings open. Her face lights up.

>   MISS CRANE (CONT'D)
>   Excuse me for a minute, will you?

Paul turns to see a somewhat HANDSOME MAN taking off his coat
and waving. She rushes to the door and greets him with a
deep kiss. Paul's smile fades. Angus comes over, concerned.

                    ANGUS
          Mr. Hunham, could you come with me,
          please?

                    PAUL
          Yeah, what is it?

Angus pulls Paul across the living room and into--

INT. MISS CRANE'S HOUSE - KITCHEN - NIGHT

-- where Mary stands by the sink, her back turned away.
Danny is next to her, trying in vain to comfort her.

Paul approaches, finding Mary weeping quietly.

                    PAUL
          Mary? Mary, are you all right?

                    MARY
          Just leave me alone.

                    DANNY
          You want me to take you home?

                    MARY
          Back off!

Stung, Danny retreats. Paul closes the door. Mary starts to
SOB.

                    MARY (CONT'D)
          He's gone.

No more brave face. Real grief in real time. The enormity
of her heartbreak leaves the men speechless.

EXT. MISS CRANE'S HOUSE - NIGHT

Supporting her on either side, Paul and Angus guide Mary down
the front steps and toward the Nova.

                    PAUL
          I was right. This is why I hate
          parties. That was a disaster.
          Total disaster!

                    ANGUS
          Speak for yourself. I was having
          fun. Let's take Mary home, make
          sure she's okay and we'll come
          back.

                    PAUL
          Out of the question.

                    ANGUS
          Would you give me a break?! I was
          hitting it off with Elise.

                    PAUL
          The niece? Are you kidding me?
          This poor woman is bereft, and all
          you can think about is some silly
          girl.

                    MARY
          I don't need you feeling sorry for
          me.

                    ANGUS
          See?! I'm just saying this is the
          first good thing that came from
          being in this prison with you.

                    PAUL
          Need I remind you it's not my fault
          you're stuck here? Do you think I
          want to be babysitting you? I was
          praying to the God I don't believe
          in that your mother would pick up
          the phone, or your father would
          arrive in a helicopter or a
          submarine or a flying fucking saucer
          to take you off my hands.

                    ANGUS
          My father's dead.

                    PAUL
          But I thought your father --

                    ANGUS
          That's just some rich guy my mom
          married. Give me your keys.

                    PAUL
          It's unlocked.

Angus heads over to open the car door.

                    MARY
          You don't tell a boy who's been
          left behind at Christmas that
          you're aching to cut him loose.
          That nobody wants him. What the
          fuck is wrong with you?

She grabs his arm.

>   MARY (CONT'D)
>   Let's go. I'm cold.

DAY 8 - CHRISTMAS DAY, 1970

INT. NURSE'S QUARTERS - EARLY MORNING

Paul lies awake, staring at the ceiling. He sits up.

INT. INFIRMARY - DAY

Now dressed, Paul looks in on Angus, still asleep.

EXT. FACULTY PARKING LOT - DAY

More snow. Paul trudges toward the Nova.

EXT. ROAD - DAY

The Nova motors past us.

EXT. CHRISTMAS TREE LOT - DAY

The Townies in orange sit drinking coffee on the hatch of a
pick-up. The Nova rattles up. Paul gets out.

>   TOWNIE #1
>   What can we do for you, chief?

>   PAUL
>   I'm looking for a tree.

>   TOWNIE #1
>   (pointing to runty trees)
>   You've come to the right place.
>   Big fire sale on all remaining
>   inventory.

EXT. ROAD - DAY

The Nova heads back to school, a small tree tied to its roof.

INT. INFIRMARY - DAY

Paul is puzzled to find the room empty.

> PAUL
> Mr. Tully? Mr. Tully? Angus
> Tully!

INT. KITCHEN - DAY

Paul enters to find Mary cooking, on the downslope of a hangover.

> PAUL
> Good morning.

> MARY
> Merry Christmas.

> PAUL
> Merry Christmas. Of course. How
> are you?

> MARY
> Got a case of the cocktail flu.

> PAUL
> Have you seen the boy?

She shakes her head.

> PAUL (CONT'D)
> Goddamn it. Where the hell can he
> be?

EXT. BARTON ACADEMY - QUAD - DAY

Paul scans the empty quad.

> PAUL
> ANGUS!

INT. STAIRWAY - HALLWAY - DAY

Now a little panicked, Paul ascends a stairway.

> PAUL
> Mr. Tully!

He hears MUSIC and follows the sound into --

INT. AUDITORIUM - CONTINUOUS

Angus plays piano. Paul listens for a few moments before making his presence known.

                    PAUL
          Merry Christmas.

                    ANGUS
          Merry Christmas.

                    PAUL
          Where the hell have you been?

                    ANGUS
          I dunno. Here.

                    PAUL
          Come on. I have something to show
          you.

INT. DINING HALL - DAY

Angus, Mary and a very proud Paul behold the bare tree, atilt in a makeshift stand. Beneath it sit three small GIFTS.

                    ANGUS
          No ornaments?

                    PAUL
          I'm sure we can round up some
          ornaments.

Paul picks up a gift and hands it to Angus.

                    PAUL (CONT'D)
          This is for you.

Angus is so surprised that he just looks at it before unwrapping it. It's a book.

                    PAUL (CONT'D)
          "Meditations" by Marcus Aurelius.
          For my money, it's like the Bible,
          the Koran and the Bhagavad Gita all
          rolled up into one. And the best
          part is not one mention of God.

                    ANGUS
          Um, okay. Thanks.

Paul gives Mary a gift.

                    PAUL
          And this is for you.

Mary opens it. It's another copy of "Meditations."

                    MARY
          So you just give this to everybody?

                    PAUL
          And--

Paul hands Mary the remaining gift. It's a badly-wrapped
bottle of whiskey.

                    MARY
          Aw. How did you guess?

                    PAUL
               (to Angus)
          Also, this came in the mail for
          you.

Paul hands Angus an envelope. He opens it. It's a card
stuffed with CASH. "Happy Holidays from Mom and Stanley."

DINING HALL - LATER

Paul, Mary and Angus finish a lovely Christmas dinner in the
middle of the immense room.

They exchange looks, a new sort of intimacy among them. Mary
lights a cigarette.

                    PAUL
          Thank you, Mary. That was just
          lovely.

                    MARY
          It that an actual compliment?

                    ANGUS
          I don't think I've ever had a real
          family Christmas like this.
          Christmas dinner, I mean -- family
          style, out of the oven, all the
          trimmings. My mom always just
          orders in from Delmonico's.

                    MARY
          She's got the right idea. Next
          year I'm ordering in from
          Delmonico's.

                    ANGUS
          Anyway. Thank you, Mary.

                    MARY
          You're welcome.

She winks at him and smiles. Paul raises a glass.

                    PAUL
          I'd like to propose a toast. To my
          two unlikely companions on this
          snowy island. And to our absent
          friends and family. I realize that
          none of us is here because he wants
          to be, so if there's anything I can
          do to make the holidays a little
          cheerier for either of you, just
          say the word.

                    ANGUS
          Okay, I want to go to Boston.

                    PAUL
          Boston. Why?

                    ANGUS
          Why not? I want a real Christmas.
          I want to go ice skating. I want
          to see a real Christmas tree with
          ornaments, not that stupid thing.

                    PAUL
          You said it was nice.

                    MARY
          It is nice.

                    ANGUS
          Come on. Let's get out of here. I
          want a real holiday.

                    PAUL
          Well, we're not going to Boston.
          It's out of the question.

                    MARY
          You just told the boy "anything."
          So take the kid to Boston.

                    PAUL
          Mary, we're not allowed to leave
          campus or the immediate environs.

Paul catches Mary and Angus's look. Sighs.

PAUL (CONT'D)
But I suppose we could call it a
field trip. A field trip would
fall under the ambit of additional
academic pursuits. There's even a
fund set aside for additional
academic pursuits.

ANGUS
I'll go pack.

Angus rises and sprints away happily.

MARY
I'm gonna need you to drive me to
Roxbury.

PAUL
All right.

HIGH AND WIDE

The Nova cruises past steepled churches and colonial
clapboard houses strung with Christmas lights. Currier &
Ives New England, snowbound and gorgeous.

The BOSTON SKYLINE comes into view.

EXT. RESIDENTIAL STREET - ROXBURY, BOSTON - DAY

The Nova pulls to the curb across from a TRIPLE-DECKER
apartment building.

INT. NOVA - CONTINUOUS

Paul puts it in park.

MARY
Here we are.

PAUL
That's an awful lot of stairs.

MARY
Probably icy, too.

Who's not getting the hint?

PAUL
Mr. Tully.

                    ANGUS
          Right. Mary, can I help with your
          bags?

                    MARY
          Yes please.

Angus gets out, opens the trunk, grabs Mary's bag and the BOX
we saw earlier.

                    MARY (CONT'D)
               (opening the window)
          Be careful with the box.

Angus carries her luggage and the Box and crosses the street.

                    PAUL
          You know you're more than welcome
          to a room at the hotel. We've got
          the money.

                    MARY
          Are you out of your mind? I need a
          break from you two and all your
          damn bickering. Besides I'm
          looking forward to visiting my
          little sister. She's pregnant.

                    PAUL
          That's wonderful.

Paul takes Mary's hand and squeezes it. She makes a face.

                    MARY
          Mr. Hunham!

                    PAUL
          Oh, sorry. My hands sweat.
          Hyperhidrosis.

Through the windshield they watch Angus navigate the stairs.
On the second level he looks down. Mary opens her door.

                    MARY
          One more flight up!
               (to Paul)
          You two going to be all right?

                    PAUL
          Oh, yes. The young monster will be
          well under control.

They see Angus summit the stairs and put the bags down.
Mary's sister PEGGY and her husband LESTER come onto the
balcony and wave.

>   PEGGY
>   Mary!

Mary's face lights up. She calls back to Peggy.

>   MARY
>   Hi!

She turns to Paul.

>   MARY (CONT'D)
>   Bye.

Mary gets out, slams the door, crosses the street and passes
Angus at the bottom of the stairs.

>   ANGUS
>   Bye, Mary.

>   MARY
>   Not yet. Now you've got to help me
>   up there.

>   ANGUS
>   Oh yeah. Sure thing.

Angus takes her arm and they begin the ascent.

INT. PEGGY'S TOWNHOUSE - GUEST BEDROOM - DAY

The room is being converted into a nursery. Someone has
started painting a wall, and there's a crib in the corner.
Mary is seated on the bed. The Box is next to her.

She stands, picks up the Box and carries it to a bureau. She
opens it, revealing OLD BABY CLOTHES. She takes out a bottle,
then a pair shoes. She holds them for a moment, smiles sadly,
then starts putting the items into the drawers.

Peggy appears in the doorway. Mary turns. They look at each
other. Mary takes a step toward her. They hug for a long
time.

INT. PEGGY'S TOWNHOUSE - GUEST BEDROOM - LATER

Mary and Peggy sit on the bed, talking and laughing. Lester
sticks his head in. The women don't notice him. He smiles
and keeps moving.

UNDER BLACK --

DAY 10 - DECEMBER 27, 1970

EXT. BOSTON STREET - DAY

Paul and Angus walk the sun-dappled, snowy streets...

EXT. ANOTHER BOSTON STREET - DAY

...through bustling crowds going about their holiday
business.

EXT. BRATTLE BOOK SHOP - DAY

Paul and Angus browse at an outdoor bookstore open even
during winter. Soon a HOOKER in a short coat and go-go boots
wanders by. She approaches Paul.

                    HOOKER
          Hi there, handsome. Got a
          cigarette?

                    PAUL
          No, sorry, I smoke a pipe.

                    HOOKER
          Then how about a date? You want a
          date?

                    PAUL
          No, thank you.

                    HOOKER
          Come on. Let's go somewhere warm.

                    ANGUS
              (to Paul)
          Go ahead. I can wait here.

                    HOOKER
          See? He can wait here and read
          some books. Get educated. He
          doesn't mind if daddy gets a little
          candy cane.

                    PAUL
          Thank you, but I've never really
          liked candy canes. Plus, I'm pre-
          diabetic.

This is hopeless. The Hooker walks away.

> ANGUS
> You know, if you do want a little
> candy cane, I won't tell anyone.

> PAUL
> Mr. Tully, for most people, sex is
> ninety-nine percent friction and one
> percent good will. Call me old-
> fashioned, but I place value on
> physical intimacy. So should you.

They leave the bookstore. Paul lights his pipe.

> ANGUS
> You've never had sex, have you?

> PAUL
> Believe it or not, Mr. Tully, there
> was a time when the fire in my
> loins burned white hot.

> ANGUS
> You're full of shit.

> PAUL
> The details would curl your toes.

> ANGUS
> Okay, we're finally getting to the
> good stuff. Let's hear.

> PAUL
> Maybe when you turn eighteen. Curl
> your toes!

INT. BOSTON FINE ARTS MUSEUM - DAY

Paul and Angus wander among ancient Greek artifacts.

> ANGUS
> Are we almost done?

> PAUL
> What's your hurry? I thought you
> liked Antiquity.

> ANGUS
> In class, maybe. But I never think
> about it unless I need to.

Paul directs Angus's attention to a display of CERAMICS.

                    PAUL
          Here. What do you see?

                    ANGUS
          I don't know. A bunch of pottery.

                    PAUL
               (pointing)
          Look at that one.

On the vase, a naked Greek couple are seriously going at it.

                    ANGUS
          Candy cane!

                    PAUL
          There's nothing new in human
          experience, Mr. Tully. Each
          generation thinks it invented
          debauchery or suffering or
          rebellion, but man's every appetite
          and impulse, from the disgusting to
          the sublime, is on display right
          here, all around you.

Paul gestures around the room, and we cut to CLOSE-UPS of the
art -- conquest, passion, sacrifice.

                    PAUL (CONT'D)
          So before you dismiss something as
          boring or irrelevant, remember that
          if you truly want to understand the
          present, or yourself, you must
          begin in the past. History is not
          merely the past, Mr. Tully. It's
          an explanation of the present.

                    ANGUS
          See, when you say it that way, and
          throw in some pornography, it's a
          lot easier to understand. You
          should try doing more of that in
          class and less yelling. You know,
          most of the kids pretty much hate
          you. Teachers, too. You know that,
          right?

Paul looks at him, then down, straining not to feel hurt.

EXT. PARK - SKATING RINK - NIGHT

Festooned for the holidays, the public rink is alive with
SKATERS.

From the sidelines, Paul watches Angus skate laps, quietly marveling at the lad's vitality.

EXT. SKATING RINK - NIGHT

Paul and Angus leave, a new ease between them.

> HUGH (O.C.)
> Paul Hunham? Is that you?

Paul turns to see a COUPLE, Paul's age, approaching at speed. They have that holiday glow.

> HUGH (CONT'D)
> Hugh. Hugh Cavanaugh.

> PAUL
> Yes, of course. Wow. Hugh Cavanaugh. How are you, Hugh?

> HUGH
> God, what's it been, thirty years? This is my wife Karen. Honey, this is Paul Hunham. We went to Harvard together.

> MRS. CAVANAUGH
> Hi, Paul.

> PAUL
>   (thrown)
> Yes, we did. Wow. So what're you up to, Hugh? Still in the area?

> HUGH
> Oh yes, still here in Boston. Cambridge.

> MRS. CAVANAUGH
> Harvard. He just got tenure. Statistics.

> HUGH
> Karen.

> MRS. CAVANAUGH
> He won't blow his own horn, so I blow it for him.

> HUGH
> Okay. What about you, Paul?

                    PAUL
Teaching as well. We have that in
common. History, ancient history.

                    HUGH
That's great. Where?

                    PAUL
Abroad mostly. On fellowships.
Privately funded fellowships.
Universities and private academies,
mostly. Fellowships. I'm
currently posted in Antwerp. Just
back here for the holidays.

                    HUGH
Is this your son?

                    ANGUS
I'm his nephew. Leonard.

                    MRS. CAVANAUGH
Nice to meet you, Leonard.

                    ANGUS
And he's writing a book right now.
Tell them about your book, Uncle
Paul.

                    PAUL
My book? It's not a book, really.
Just a monograph. Nothing special.

                    ANGUS
Don't be so modest. It's about,
uh, cameras, right? Ancient
cameras.

                    HUGH
Huh.

                    PAUL
What he means, of course, is the
camera obscura. You know, the
optical and astronomical tool that
dates back to, um, the time of
Anaxagoras.

                    ANGUS
Tell him the title, Uncle Paul.

                    PAUL
He's not interested, Leonard.

                    HUGH
Sure I am.

                    PAUL
"Light and Magic in The Ancient
World."

                    HUGH
Well, Paul, I'm so glad you landed
on your feet. You look swell.

                    PAUL
You too. So swell.

                    HUGH
And we'll keep an eye out for your
book. Won't we, honey?

                    MRS. CAVANAUGH
Of course. Merry Christmas, Paul.
Bye, Leonard.

                    ANGUS
Merry Christmas.

Paul's forced jocularity vanishes, and he marches away.

                    ANGUS (CONT'D)
What the fuck just happened?

Paul just keeps walking.

INT. LIQUOR STORE - NIGHT

Paul enters and starts scanning the shelves. Angus follows.

                    ANGUS
I thought Barton men don't lie.
Don't get me wrong, that was fun,
but you just lied through your
teeth.

                    PAUL
What I say during a private
conversation is none of your
goddamn business. You're not to
judge me.

                    ANGUS
It wasn't a private conversation.
The wife and I were there. And I
helped you. Why'd he ask if you
landed on your feet?

                    PAUL
          What is this, Nuremberg?

                    ANGUS
          You're the hard-ass constantly
          telling everybody not to lie and
          going on and on about the honor
          code.

                    PAUL
          There was an incident when I was at
          Harvard. With my roommate.

                    ANGUS
          And?

                    PAUL
          He accused me of copying from his
          senior thesis. Plagiarizing.

                    ANGUS
          Well, did you?

                    PAUL
          No! He stole from *me*. But that
          blue-blooded prick's family had
          allies on the faculty -- I mean,
          their last name is on a library --
          so he accused *me* in order to
          sanitize his treachery. And they
          threw me out.

                    ANGUS
          So you got kicked out of Harvard
          for cheating?

                    PAUL
          No. I got kicked out of Harvard
          for hitting him.

                    ANGUS
          You hit him? Like punched him out?

                    PAUL
          No, I hit him with a car.

                    ANGUS
          You got kicked out of Harvard for
          hitting a guy with a car?!

Paul finally sees his Jim Beam behind the register and
approaches the stone-faced CASHIER.

                    PAUL
          By accident. But he broke three
          ribs. Which was technically his
          fault, because he shouldn't have
          been in the road. Pint of Jim
          Beam.

                    CASHIER
          Two dollars, please.

Paul pulls out his wallet and pays the Cashier.

                    PAUL
               (to Angus)
          Also, he shat himself, which was
          the greater indignity.

                    CASHIER
               (handing him the bottle)
          Here you go, killer.

EXT. BOSTON STREET - CONTINUOUS

They exit the liquor store and walk around the corner.

                    ANGUS
          So Mr. Hunham never even graduated
          college? Holy shit. You didn't
          finish up somewhere else?

Paul gives him a look -- *"I'm more mysterious than you
thought."* He cracks open the pint of Jim. Takes a pull.

                    ANGUS (CONT'D)
          Who else knows?

                    PAUL
          Dr. Green knew. Only Dr. Green.
          He'd always believed in me, so he
          gave me a job. Adjunct faculty --
          zero respect and even less pay, so
          nobody batted an eye -- and I've
          been at the school ever since.

                    ANGUS
          Are you ashamed how things turned
          out?

                    PAUL
          Not at all. I'm proud of my work.
          I love history, I love Barton.
          Barton is my life. I don't know
          what I'd do without Barton.

> ANGUS
> Then why did you lie to that guy?

> PAUL
> Because I knew he'd relish the fact that I'm a washout and never left my own high school. And he'd probably repeat that story to everybody we used to know. So I figured he's not entitled to my story. I am.

> ANGUS
> Yeah. Fuck that guy.

> PAUL
> Exactly. Fuck that guy.
> (mocking)
> *Statistics.*
> (quiet panic)
> But you'll keep this quiet, right? No one is to know. I mean no one, Angus.

> ANGUS
> *Entre nous,* sir. *Entre nous.*

A moment later --

> PAUL
> Ancient cameras? Where the hell'd you come up with that?

> ANGUS
> Just trying to keep you on your toes, sir.

UNDER BLACK --

DAY 11 - DECEMBER 28, 1970

INT. HOTEL ROOM - MORNING

Angus awakens to find Paul fully dressed.

> PAUL
> Get up, kid. It's daylight in the swamp.

Angus swings his legs out of bed. Paul gestures to a ROOM SERVICE TRAY.

                    PAUL (CONT'D)
          I ordered breakfast.

                    ANGUS
          Great.

Angus grabs something out of his suitcase but drops it on the
way to the bathroom -- a BOTTLE OF PILLS. Paul picks it up.

                    ANGUS (CONT'D)
          Those are my vitamins.

                    PAUL
          Librium?

                    ANGUS
          Yeah, it's just something I'm
          supposed to take. For low energy.

                    PAUL
          You mean depression?

                    ANGUS
          Hey, is that rye toast? How'd you
          know I like rye toast?

Angus grabs a slice and disappears into the bathroom. Paul
reaches into his suitcase, pulls out a BOTTLE OF LIBRIUM of
his own, and unscrews the cap.

INT. CANDLEPIN BOWLING ALLEY - DAY

There's a BAR inside, and Christmas decorations. LOCALS
laugh, drink, bowl.

AT A LANE

Paul rolls. Okay, but not great. Rolls again. Meh.

Angus rolls. Spare. Rolls again. Strike!

Paul rolls again. So-so.

                    ANGUS
          You're not very good at this.

                    PAUL
          Your grasp of the obvious is
          remarkable.

                    ANGUS
          It's your form. Just hold on
          tightly, then let go lightly.

Paul glares, then tries it. Much better.

>   PAUL
>   You're a pretty good teacher, kid.
>   Too bad everyone dislikes you.
>   Pretty much hates you. But you
>   must know that, right?

>   ANGUS
>   Touché, sir. Touché.

Angus notices a LOCAL GIRL smiling at him from a nearby lane.
Her GIRLFRIEND whispers to her. They laugh. Angus doesn't
quite know how to take this.

>   ANGUS (CONT'D)
>   Which eye do you aim with, anyway?
>   You know, I've been meaning to ask.
>   When we're talking, which eye
>   should I look at? Sometimes I look
>   at one, then I think I'm wrong, so
>   I look at the other one.

>   PAUL
>   Everybody does that.

>   ANGUS
>   So which eye is it?

Paul just smiles before lifting his ball for another roll.

LATER - AT THE BAR

A bourbon lands in front of Paul. He takes a big slug.

In the distance, Angus now bowls with the girls. Paul shoots
amused looks at Angus before losing himself in reverie.

Drinking and smoking a few barstools away is a gin-blossomed
SANTA chatting with the BARTENDER.

>   BARTENDER
>   People don't understand. This
>   isn't tenpin. It's much harder.
>   All these tenpin assholes coming in
>   here like they're slumming it, to
>   hell with them.

>   SANTA CLAUS
>   Yeah, fuck 'em.

Paul lights his pipe and leans towards them, full of
bonhomie.

> PAUL
> Here's something I'll bet you
> didn't know. Your uniform, festive
> as it is, is historically
> inaccurate. St. Nicholas of Myra
> was actually a 4th-century Greek
> bishop from what is now Turkey, so
> a robe and sandals would be closer
> to the mark. But I guess that
> would be impractical, given the
> weather, and, of course, all the
> silly -- but lucrative -- mythology
> about Santa Claus and elves and
> reindeer and chimneys and what not.
> Still, what can you do? As
> Democritus said: "World is decay.
> Life is perception."

Paul puffs on his pipe, satisfied. The Bartender and Santa
just stare at him. Who is this pedantic asshole?

INT. MOVIE THEATRE BALCONY

Paul and Angus watch "Little Big Man," popcorn between them.

> PAUL
> This is not only amusing, but for a
> movie, it's a fairly accurate
> depiction of life among the
> Cheyenne.

> NEARBY PATRON
> Shhhh.

> PAUL
> Fuck off.

> ANGUS
> I'm going to the bathroom.

Paul nods.

INT. MOVIE THEATRE LOBBY - DAY

Angus walks downstairs from the balcony, but rather than
heading for the bathroom, he chooses the front doors.

INT. MOVIE THEATRE - DAY

Engrossed by the film, Paul suddenly glances in alarm at
Angus's empty seat.

EXT. MOVIE THEATRE - DAY

Paul emerges from the theater just in time to catch Angus climbing into a TAXI.

> PAUL
> Hey! Hey!

He sprints toward Angus, who slams the door shut. Paul opens it.

> PAUL (CONT'D)
> Get out.

> ANGUS
> I just need to do something. I was going to come back. Or meet you at the hotel. It won't take long. It's nothing bad.

> PAUL
> Get out, you conniving little shit!

Angus stays put.

> PAUL (CONT'D)
> Were you planning this the whole time? Just counting the minutes until I turned my back?

> ANGUS
> I'm not running away. There's just something I need to do before we go back to school. Please.
>   (then)
> You could come with me. Just come with me, okay?

> PAUL
> Come with you where?

> ANGUS
> To see my dad.

> PAUL
> Your dad? That's what this is about? Why didn't you just ask me? Because of course we can go to a cemetery.

EXT. PSYCHIATRIC HOSPITAL DRIVEWAY - DAY

Through the taxi windshield, we motor up a long access road.

EXT. PSYCHIATRIC HOSPITAL - DAY

The taxi arrives at a large stone building.

INT. PSYCHIATRIC HOSPITAL CORRIDOR - DAY

An ORDERLY leads Angus and Paul up stairs and toward a door.

A look passes between Angus and Paul. Angus enters alone.
Paul sits on a nearby bench.

INT. PSYCHIATRIC HOSPITAL DAY ROOM - DAY

A large, bright space for supervised visits. A couple of
OTHER PATIENTS have visitors, too.

The Orderly enters with THOMAS TULLY, 50ish. He's wearing
hospital garb and his eyes have that glazed Thorazine look.
The Orderly steers him towards Angus.

            ANGUS
   Hi, Dad.

            THOMAS
   Hello, sweetheart.

Angus embraces him.

            ANGUS
   You want to sit down for a little?

Thomas doesn't respond. Confusion in his eyes. The Orderly
guides him to a table.

            ORDERLY
   Sit right here. There you go.

Father and son sit across from each other.

            ANGUS
   I've missed you. I've missed you a
   lot. A whole lot. You know, I'm
   still in school. At Barton. And
   it's Christmastime now, so I
   thought you'd like a visit.

Thomas stares at him. Angus nervously fills the silence.

            ANGUS (CONT'D)
   Guess what? I'm actually keeping my
   grades up.
          (MORE)

                    ANGUS (CONT'D)
I consistently get the highest
grades in the class in Ancient Civ.
And I'm pretty much third or fourth
in Precalculus. And I'm in the
chess club, but I don't really like
the other kids. And in the spring
I'm going to try out for tennis.
Just JV, and probably only doubles,
if the coach can just forget about
my... anyway, not important.

                    THOMAS
I want to tell you something.

Thomas takes his hand. Angus leans forward eagerly,
listening.

                    THOMAS (CONT'D)
I think they're putting something
in my food.

EXT. HIGHWAY - NIGHT

A TAXI heads back toward Boston. It's snowing. Angus gazes
sadly out the window. Paul sits beside him, watching him.

INT. FANCY RESTAURANT - NIGHT

Angus sits across the table from Paul.

                    ANGUS
He used to be fine. Better than
fine. He was great. He was my
dad. Then about four years ago, he
started acting strange - like,
erratic, forgetful, saying all this
weird shit. My mom took him to a
bunch of doctors, and they put him
on medication. But that just made
it worse. He got more confused.
And then he got angry, and then he
got... physical. And that was the
last straw. They put him away.
Then she divorced him. Without him
even realizing it. That's why she
wants a whole new life. And it's
easy to just stash me away in a
boarding school, like half of us
there are just stashed away. And I
get it -- she never has to look at
me, because when she looks at me,
she sees him.

                    PAUL
          That can't be true. You're her son.

                    ANGUS
          And she's right. I can't keep it
          together. I lie. I steal. I piss
          people off. I don't have any
          friends, real friends. I'll
          probably get kicked out of Barton
          too, and when I do, it'll be my own
          fault. I'll get sent to Fork
          Union, and then maybe to you-know-
          where, and nobody will care. The
          funny thing is, I wanted to see my
          dad so bad, but I also didn't.
          Because I'm afraid that's what's
          going to happen to me one day.

                    PAUL
          Angus, listen. You're not your
          father.

                    ANGUS
          How do you know?

                    PAUL
          Because no one is his own father.
          I'm not my dad, no matter how hard
          he tried to beat that idea into me.

Paul trails off, stares into space. Angus takes note.

                    PAUL (CONT'D)
          I find the world a bitter and
          complicated place, and it seems to
          feel the same way about me. I
          think you and I have this in
          common. Don't get me wrong -- you
          have your challenges. You're
          erratic and belligerent and a
          gigantic pain in the balls, but
          you're not me, and you're not your
          father. You're your own man. Man.
          No. You're just a kid. You're
          just beginning. And you're smart.
          You've got time to turn things
          around.

Angus absorbs this wide-eyed, like a benediction.

                    PAUL (CONT'D)
Sure, the Greeks had the idea that
the steps you take to avoid your
fate are the very steps that lead
to it, but that's just a literary
conceit. In real life, your
history does not have to dictate
your desti --
          (noticing)
Oh, here's Mary.

                    ANGUS
Can you not tell Mary, or anybody,
about --

                    PAUL
Entre nous. This whole damn trip
is *entre nous*. Stand up.

                    ANGUS
What?

                    PAUL
Stand up for the lady, you boor.
You cretin.

Mary approaches the table. They stand as Mary sits.

                    MARY
Thank you. Sorry I'm late.

                    PAUL
We're just happy to see you.

                    HOST
Madame, your menu.

The host leaves, and shortly the WAITRESS approaches.

                    WAITRESS
Hello, ma'am. Would you like a
cocktail to start?

                    MARY
I'll just have tea, please. And
I've eaten.

                    PAUL
Have a cocktail.

                    MARY
Just a cup of tea.

                    WAITRESS
          And you, gentlemen? Did you save
          room for dessert?

A WAITER at a nearby table sets fire to a chafing dish. A
YOUNG COUPLE marvels at the spectacle.

                    ANGUS
          What's that?

                    WAITRESS
          That's our signature dessert.
          Cherries jubilee.

                    ANGUS
          That sounds great.

                    PAUL
          Bring the young vandal here
          cherries jubilee.

                    WAITRESS
          I'm afraid I can't. The dish
          contains brandy. Same deal with
          the bananas foster.

                    MARY
          But all the alcohol burns off,
          right?

                    WAITRESS
          It's still against the rules,
          ma'am.

                    PAUL
          Fine. I'll order the cherries
          jubilee. We can share it.

                    WAITRESS
          I can't allow that either.

                    MARY
          What if it's his birthday?

                    ANGUS
          It's my birthday.

                    WAITRESS
          Happy birthday, young man. Let's
          get you a slice of cake or some
          other age-appropriate dessert.

                    PAUL
          Christ on a crutch, what kind of
          fascist hash foundry are you
          running here?

                    MARY
          Let me ask you a question. Do you
          have cherries?

                    WAITRESS
          Yes.

                    MARY
          Great. And do you have ice cream?

                    WAITRESS
          Yes.

                    MARY
          Fantastic. Can we please get
          cherries and ice cream to go?

                    PAUL
          And the check.

                    WAITRESS
          Right away.

The Waitress leaves in a snit.

                    MARY
               (as the Waitress leaves)
          Bitch.

EXT. FANCY RESTAURANT PARKING LOT - NIGHT

Paul, Angus and Mary stand before a TAKEOUT CONTAINER atop
the trunk of a car. Mary has a cigarette in her mouth and
matches in her hand.

                    ANGUS
          I swiped us spoons.

                    PAUL
          I don't approve, but good thinking.

                    MARY
          Hurry up. I'm cold.

Paul unscrews his flask and soaks the cherries a little too
much.

                         PAUL
             James Beam....

Mary lights a match and touches it to the cherries. FLAMES.

                         PAUL (CONT'D)
             Presto! Cherries jubilee!

The flames shoot up so much that the takeout container
catches fire.

                         ANGUS
             Shit! Shit!

                         MARY
             How much alcohol did you put on
             there?

WIDE

LAUGHTER as they knock the flaming container onto the
pavement and struggle to extinguish the blaze.

EXT. NEW ENGLAND ROAD - DAY

The Nova heads home.

INT. NOVA - DAY

The threesome ride home in silence, and we observe each of
them in close-up. Each smiles faintly.

INT. KITCHEN STAFF COMMON ROOM - NIGHT

Paul, Angus, Mary and Danny cluster around the TV -- GUY
LOMBARDO AND HIS ROYAL CANADIANS.

                         MARY
             We should have noise-makers.

                         ANGUS
             I've got a noise-maker.

Angus produces an M-80 from his pocket.

                         PAUL
             Where the hell did you get that?

                         ANGUS
             I don't know. Found it.

                         PAUL
          You're not deploying that in here.

                         ANGUS
          You weren't this uptight in Boston.
          Danny, where do you stand on indoor
          fireworks?

                         DANNY
          About as far away as I can.

THE COUNTDOWN to 1971 begins. They turn to watch.

                         EVERYONE
          Three, two, one. Happy New Year!

Paul shakes everyone's hand.

                         PAUL
          Congratulations, Mr. Tully.
          Congratulations, Danny. Mary.
               (holding up M-80)
          Now, as I say, we're not deploying
          this in here. We're going to light
          this sucker off in the kitchen.

EXT. KITCHEN STAFF COMMON ROOM - CONTINUOUS

They head to the adjacent kitchen area. Paul gives the M-80
to Angus and lights it for him. Angus throws it off-screen.
LOUD EXPLOSION.

Through the windows we see the threesome hugging one another.

                                        FADE OUT

UNDER BLACK --

               NEW SEMESTER - JANUARY 11, 1971

EXT. QUAD - DAY

The CROSS-COUNTRY TEAM races across the quad in watch caps
and grey sweats.

INT. WEIGHT ROOM - DAY

The Barton CREW cranks away on indoor rowing machines as the
COACH keeps the cadence, urging them on.

INT. NEW GYMNASIUM - DAY

The BASKETBALL TEAM runs drills on the new gym floor.

INT. STUDENT DORMITORY - DAY

Boys dress, laugh, fight. Two play lacrosse in the hall.
Smith steps from the shower, toweling his FRESHLY-CUT hair.

INT. KITCHEN - DAY

The cooks are back at work. Mary checks the seasoning on a
big pot of soup.

> MARY
> This is too much paprika. Why did
> you put in all that paprika?
> Follow the recipe. Now you've got
> to add a third cup of water. Come
> on.

INT. PAUL'S CLASSROOM - DAY

Angus and the rest await the start of class. Kountze is
terribly sunburned except for the outline of his goggles.

> CROCKER
> Hey Kountze: does it still hurt?

> KOUNTZE
> Fuck yeah, it hurts. Glare off the
> slopes, man. Burned me to a crisp.
>   (off Angus's laugh)
> You think it's funny, Tully?

> ANGUS
> No, man. I'm just glad you had a
> good vacation.

> PAUL
>   (sweeping in)
> Welcome back, you snarling
> Visigoths. I trust you all enjoyed
> a refreshing holiday.
>   (noticing)
> Oh, hello, Mr. Kountze. Or should
> I say Icarus? Fly a little too
> close to the sun, did we?

> KOUNTZE
> Huh?

>   PAUL
>   All right, everyone. Along with
>   your skiing and swimming, I hope
>   you found time to enlighten
>   yourselves about the Peloponnesian
>   War and its implications for today.
>   Just to check, we're going to start
>   with a short pop quiz on the
>   reading before we retake the final
>   from last semester. *Omnia ex
>   scrineis vestris praeter stilum.*

The boys groan and put their books on the ground. Angus and
Paul share a conspiratorial smile.

EXT. ADMINISTRATION BUILDING - DAY

A shiny Cadillac pulls up and parks. Out step a WELL-GROOMED
COUPLE, and they head inside.

INT. PAUL'S CLASSROOM - DAY

Paul sits alone at his desk, correcting exams. Miss Crane
opens the door.

>   MISS CRANE
>   Excuse me, Mr. Hunham.

>   PAUL
>   Miss Crane. Lydia. Come in.
>   Happy New Year.

>   MISS CRANE
>   Same to you. Happy new year.

>   PAUL
>   Forgive me. I'm a clod. I never
>   called to thank you for inviting
>   the boy and me to your party. And
>   Mary. It meant a lot.

>   MISS CRANE
>   You're so welcome. It was fun.
>   Um, Dr. Woodrup is asking to see
>   you. He says it's urgent.

INT. HEADMASTER'S OUTER OFFICE - DAY

As Miss Crane and Paul arrive, Paul is surprised to find
Angus seated in the waiting area. Their eyes meet.

Miss Crane opens Woodrup's door, and a puzzled Paul crosses the threshold, still looking at Angus.

Miss Crane closes the door, glances at Angus, then hurries away down the corridor.

INT. HEADMASTER'S OFFICE - CONTINUOUS

Dr. Woodrup sits across from the Well-Groomed Couple.

>   DR. WOODRUP
>   Mr. Hunham, meet Judy and Stanley
>   Clotfelter, Angus Tully's mother
>   and father.

>   STANLEY
>   Stepfather.

>   JUDY
>   Hello.

>   PAUL
>   Good morning.

>   DR. WOODRUP
>   They've brought something very
>   important to my attention.

>   STANLEY
>   We understand you took Angus to
>   Boston over the holidays.

>   DR. WOODRUP
>   I explained to Mr. Clotfelter that
>   you went on a field trip. For
>   academic reasons.

>   PAUL
>   That's right.

>   JUDY
>   A field trip.

>   PAUL
>   Yes, as per my instructions in the
>   manual, it fell within the ambit of
>   my responsibility.

>   STANLEY
>   If it was a school trip, then how
>   do you explain this?

Stanley reaches into his coat and places the SNOW GLOBE atop Woodrup's desk. It's the same one we saw Angus playing with at Miss Crane's Christmas party.

>   JUDY
>   The people at the sanitarium
>   confiscated it from my ex-husband.
>   Apparently Angus had given it to
>   him.

INT. HEADMASTER'S OUTER OFFICE - DAY

Angus overhears his fate being decided by muffled voices. Miss Crane returns, now accompanied by Mary in her kitchen whites and hairnet.

>   ANGUS
>   My mother and Stanley are here.

>   MARY
>   Lydia told me.

>   ANGUS
>   I think I'm going to get kicked
>   out. And that means military
>   school.

Miss Crane turns and leaves. Mary looks at Angus long and hard, then sits next to him, and takes his hand.

INT. HEADMASTER'S OFFICE - DAY

The reckoning continues.

>   JUDY
>   Angus knows he isn't supposed to
>   see his father. He suffers from
>   debilitating mental illnesses --
>   paranoid schizophrenia, early onset
>   dementia. And Angus's visit
>   created an expectation. Tom wants
>   to come home now, which is clearly
>   impossible. They tried to explain
>   that to him, and he --

>   STANLEY
>   (picking up snow globe)
>   He got violent. Tried to brain one
>   of the orderlies with this goddamn
>   thing.
>   (MORE)

                    STANLEY (CONT'D)
Look, you people know the boy has a
discipline problem, and if this is
what you call supervision --

                    DR. WOODRUP
Paul, the Clotfelters want to
withdraw Angus from Barton and
enroll him at Fork Union Military
Academy.

                    STANLEY
It'll set him straight once and for
all. He could do a lot worse than
a career in the military.

                    JUDY
Stanley.

Judy holds up a hand to quiet Stanley.

                    JUDY (CONT'D)
Look, Angus has defied me lots of
times about a lot of things,
including this. So however he
manipulated your sympathies or
slipped the leash, just tell us.

The Clotfelters and Dr. Woodrup look at Paul expectantly for
a long beat. Then:

                    PAUL
It was my idea.
   (off everyone's stare)
He didn't trick me or slip the
leash. I took him to see his
father. In fact, I convinced him
to do so.

                    JUDY
This is a family matter. You had
no right to interfere.

                    PAUL
I don't give a shit.

                    DR. WOODRUP
Hunham!

                    PAUL
I said I don't give a shit. You
two were unreachable. He was all
alone at Christmas. I just thought
the kid should see his father.

> JUDY
> Do you understand what you've done?
> I have to move Tom now. It was
> hard even finding a facility that
> would take him, and now I have to
> move him.

> PAUL
> And that is deeply unfortunate.
> But why compound the misery by
> ruining the boy? I just spent two
> solid weeks with him. He's a pain
> in the ass, sure, but he's also
> really smart. I don't know about
> brilliant, but really smart. You
> must know that. He's got enormous
> potential. It would be devastating
> if you pulled him out now.

INT. HEADMASTER'S OUTER OFFICE - DAY

Mary and Angus wait, holding hands. They hear approaching
footsteps.

INT. HEADMASTER'S OFFICE - CONTINUOUS

Dr. Woodrup opens the door. Paul slowly walks over and joins
Woodrup at the threshold.

> DR. WOODRUP
> You did this to yourself, Hunham.
> Not me. I want you to remember
> that.

> PAUL
> Hardy, I have known you since you
> were a boy, so I think I have the
> requisite experience and insight to
> aver that you are, and always have
> been, penis cancer in human form.

EXT. HEADMASTER'S OFFICE - CONTINUOUS

Paul emerges. He looks squarely at Angus. Then at Mary.
Again at Angus. Angus searches Paul's face. Finally, Paul
points to an eye.

> PAUL
> It's this one. This is the one you
> should look at.

Paul smiles thinly. Angus smiles back. As Paul walks away,
the office door opens again.

> DR. WOODRUP
> Angus, step inside, please.

ON PAUL, as he continues walking.

> DISSOLVE TO:

INT. FACULTY RESIDENCE - PAUL'S ROOM - DAY

The place is largely emptied out. Paul is packing a box. In
one box is a stack of copies of "Meditations."

Mary appears in the doorway.

> MARY
> I missed you at breakfast.

> PAUL
> I was busy.

> MARY
> Have you decided where you're going
> to go?

> PAUL
> Yes and no. First I'm going to
> stash my stuff at a friend's in
> Syracuse. Then... I don't know.
> Maybe I'll start in Carthage.

> MARY
> I was hoping you'd say that.

She hands him a small gift. He opens it. It's a leather-
bound NOTEBOOK. He's touched.

> MARY (CONT'D)
> For your monograph.

> PAUL
> (flipping through)
> I don't know, Mary. There are a
> lot of empty pages in here.

> MARY
> That's your problem, man. Just
> write one word after the other.
> How hard can that be?

                  PAUL
What about you?

                  MARY
What about me what? I'm not going
anywhere. I'm not like you. I
like having a job. And now I'm
saving up for college.
     (off his look)
My sister's baby.

                  PAUL
And what is the word from Penny?

                  MARY
Peggy. Only that if it's a boy,
his middle names's going to be
Curtis.

EXT. REAR OF FACULTY RESIDENCE - DAY

Carrying a box to the parking lot, Paul passes a GROUP OF
BOYS -- Smith included -- playing grab-ass football.

On the margins, Kountze, Angus and Park watch him pack up his
U-HAUL TRAILER.

                KOUNTZE
I hear he got booted for eating
feces.

                  PARK
What?

                KOUNTZE
Yeah, apparently he got caught in
the locker room with his hand in
the commode, burgling turds.

Angus doesn't take his eyes off Paul.

                ANGUS
That's not what I heard.

                  PARK
Yeah? What did you hear?

TIGHT ON Kountze.

                KOUNTZE
Doesn't matter. Either way, he's
history. Fucker taught history,
now is history. Right, Tully?

WIDE - Angus is no longer there.

EXT. FACULTY PARKING LOT - DAY

Paul loads the last box. He slams the door to the U-Haul shut. Angus is there.

> ANGUS
> Hi.

> PAUL
> Oh, hi.

They look at each other a moment.

> ANGUS
> I don't know what you said to my mom and Stanley and Woodrup. All I know is I'm not getting kicked out. And you got fired.

> PAUL
> I just told the truth. Mostly.

> ANGUS
> Barton man.

> PAUL
> Barton man.

The BELL rings.

> PAUL (CONT'D)
> That's fifth period.

Reflexively, Angus takes a couple steps away, then turns.

> ANGUS
> You know, it's only PE. Maybe I could skip it, and we could head over to the Winning Ticket, grab a burger and a beer?

> PAUL
> A Miller High Life, no doubt. You never give up, do you?

> ANGUS
> Well, they already fired you, so I figured it was worth a shot.

> PAUL
> Your logic is flawless. But no.

They look at each other a long moment.

>   PAUL (CONT'D)
>   Keep your head up, all right? You
>   can do this.

>   ANGUS
>   I was gonna tell you the same
>   thing.

They lock eyes. They want to hug, but instead they just
SHAKE HANDS. Angus abruptly starts running back to campus.

>   ANGUS (CONT'D)
>   (over his shoulder)
>   See 'ya.

>   PAUL
>   See 'ya.

Paul watches him go until he disappears inside the building,
and then stares after him for a moment or two longer.

EXT. BARTON CAMPUS - DAY

The Nova, towing the U-Haul, drives past the Main Hall.

INT. NOVA - DAY

THROUGH THE WINDSHIELD

The gothic buildings recede in the distance as Paul
approaches the back gate.

Paul's face reveals the terror and hope he feels at leaving
the only home he's ever known.

EXT. BARTON DRIVEWAY / FRONT GATE - DAY

He stops at the edge of the road.

INT. NOVA - DAY

INSIDE THE CAR

Paul reaches into a box and pulls out Woodrup's CRYSTAL
BOTTLE of Louis XIII. He uncorks it, takes a swig, swishes
it around like mouthwash and spits it out the window.
Blinker on, he cautiously pulls out onto the road, then steps
on the gas.

HIGH AND WIDE

The camera holds on the Nova as it speeds away, disappearing
in the distance.

THE END

Made in the USA
Las Vegas, NV
08 May 2024

89647002R00063